The Magic of
Make Believe

Beyond Positive Thinking

D0836128

The Magic of Make Believe

Beyond Positive Thinking

Lee Pascoe

FINDHORN
Press

First published in English by Findhorn Press 2006
First published in French under the title *Faites Comme Si!*
© Le Courrier du Livre 2004

ISBN 10: 1-84409-075-2
ISBN 13: 978-1-84409-075-4

British Library Cataloguing-in-Publication Data.
A catalogue record for this book is available
from the British Library.

Edited by Judy Rickard
Cover and interior design by Damian Keenan
Printed and bound by WS Bookwell, Finland

Published by
Findhorn Press
305a The Park, Findhorn
Forres IV36 3TE
Scotland, UK

Telephone
01309 - 690582
Fax
01309 - 690036

info@findhornpress.com
www.findhornpress.com

Contents

Prologue

It was the last day of school, and we were about to be sent off from this protected clime to the real world outside. We were 16-year-old school-girls about to become adults. Exams were over, studies were finished. Most teachers simply supervised us while we played games or read comics to while away the last few official hours of school.

Then Miss Beckwith arrived. She was our English teacher, in some ways a stereotypical spinster school-ma'am, devoted to her girls. Her no-nonsense approach always prevented discussion from straying from the academic subject at hand.

"Put away your games, girls; we're going to have a talk. Tell me, what do you want to be? Not what job; what do *you*, personally, want to *be*?"

We were a bit perplexed. Talk about our personal lives? In class?

"Come along; if you could be or do anything you wanted, what would that be?"

The first responses were giggly and flighty. "Blonde and gorgeous" provoked laughter all round. But eventually we started to warm to the subject and responded: "A nice person." "More confident." "Clever." "Motivated to study harder." "Without my lousy temper." "Happy." We hardly noticed the time as we shared our personal fantasies with each other and with Miss Beckwith. Then the bell rang and we automatically started to pick up our games and novels.

"Just a minute," said Miss Beckwith, "I haven't dismissed you yet."

We looked up, surprised.

"We haven't quite finished. Now you've all talked about what you want to be. What are you going to do about it?" She waited just a second or so, looking at us intently. "Well, now, be it! What's stopping you? You can be whoever you want to be. So...just *be it*! And don't wait until you grow up. Start now. Goodbye, girls, and good luck!"

Thirty years later, I appreciate what she was trying to give us, her final treasured gift, before sending us out into the world from the safety of the nest. She wanted us to understand, somewhere in the whirlwind that is the adolescent mind, that nothing could stop us, except our own belief, or lack of it.

"Only believe..." How many times have we *wanted* to believe, but couldn't?

We can *create* our belief. We can, quite literally, Make Believe.

This little book is the result of a lifetime of working with different belief systems. It is offered to all those who have tried hard to believe in a more positive, fulfilled, happy life – and have seemingly failed.

Help is at hand.

Introduction

CHAPTER 1

Make Believe

I imagine you have this book in your hand because you are interested in personal development, in changing your life for the better. Perhaps you have found it in the Self-Help or the Psychology section of your bookshop, or perhaps it has been lent to you by a friend.

Already, you would like to believe that you will find help or inspiration in these pages, but perhaps you have doubts. This is normal! And it doesn't matter! With this system, *you don't have to believe* in what you want to have happen.

Doubtless you have already come across umpteen different books, articles and courses, all of which teach the same basic tenet: "You must believe!"

... "Anything the mind can believe, the mind can achieve."
... "Only believe, and you will be healed."
... "With faith you can move mountains."
... "If you believe positive things will happen, you will attract them into your life."
... "Believe you can succeed, and you will succeed."
... "Believe you are the greatest."

This is all very well, but how do you believe the unbelievable? Belief cannot be forced, especially when it is supposed to be true belief.

In the New Testament, Mark recounts how a man brings his son to Jesus, after the disciples have failed to cast out the demon from him. Jesus tells him all things are possible if he can only believe. The father cries out in desperation, "Lord, I believe! help thou mine unbelief!" (Mark 9:24)

This cry has echoed down the centuries, ringing out from every one of us who recognises the importance of belief, and our weak capacity to do so:

"I want to believe, but I can't! How can I? Help me!"

In this little book, I am going to offer you a solution, which may shock you. Don't even try to believe! Just pretend – Make Believe it's so! If this seems bizarre, or artificial, or even immoral, please just keep an open mind and carry on reading...

To be sure, the very words "make believe" imply that you are not serious or genuine. At best, it's just fooling around; at worst, it's false. In fact, the Americans are quite brash about it: "Fake it till you make it!"

On the other hand the word "believe" is considered extremely important and serious, a very solemn undertaking. Apart from the importance accorded to belief in religious writings throughout the centuries, tomes of modern self-help books have been written on the subject. Saints and sinners have struggled to have faith – to be true believers.

Perhaps these common distinctions need to be re-thought. What is it to "make believe"? If we break it down into its components we discover that it means, literally, to create your own belief.

Believing is supposed to be serious stuff, so if you can't do it right, better not do it at all. But "make believe" is just playing, so we are permitted to indulge in a little fun, a little fantasy. When you "make believe", you allow yourself, just temporarily, to believe the unbelievable. And therein you have a *stunningly powerful tool. This is the secret of overcoming your mental barriers.*

Every time that you start to entertain the idea that you can be better than you are and then say "But I can't believe it! It's not real!" you are blocking yourself. Your rational mind is preventing you from making a mistake, and you stay exactly where you are, within the barriers of your disbelief. But when you make believe, you dissolve the barriers. You know it's not real, but you do it anyway. After all, it's only make believe; you're just pretending. Even your logical, rational mind can accept that, and go along, at least temporarily, for the ride.

Make Believe

We know that "wishing is not believing." But "making believe" is not wishful thinking. When you wish, you sit back and do nothing, retreating into your fantasy world. When you make believe, you plunge into action. You allow yourself to do, say and feel new experiences, by playing a role.

And what are the results? The pretence becomes reality. You see measurable, regular effects in your daily life. What was accepted, although not real at the time, eventually becomes real, through the amazing magic of make believe.

At this point you are probably saying to yourself, "This is all very well and good, but is it anything more than just another motivational hype for positive thinking?"

No. This is *beyond* positive thinking. Make believe picks up where positive thinking leaves off.

Positive thinking usually fails when we try to convince ourselves we actually believe something we know is not true. Instead of creating belief, we create conflict. We try to blast through concrete barriers instead of opening a door and walking through.

Changing belief systems can be extremely difficult. Even scientists, when faced with irrefutable new evidence, will often refuse to believe their own eyes, as the existing belief structure or paradigm is both powerful and rigid. It may take a great deal of time, and repeated proof, to convince them to shift their perception of reality. You, however, can shift your perceptions immediately by making believe.

To use the wall as a metaphor for a block in your life, let's look at the difference between trying to believe and making believe:

(a) Trying to believe: "There is no wall... This wall doesn't exist... I'll just... Ouch! That hurt! This isn't working!"

(b) Making Believe: "If there were no wall, I wonder what it would be like on the other side... I'll just pretend I'm over on the other side having a great time... Isn't this fun?"

In other words, if you charge headlong against reality, you will get a nasty shock. If you play with the idea of *what it would be like if...*, then the apparent barriers simply dissolve.

Let's look at a more practical example, for a weight problem:

(a) Trying to believe: "I'm not fat... I'm not fat... I'm slim and attractive. Oh, look at that stomach! How depressing! I think I'll have another chocolate cake to cheer up. Bother, I've failed again. I knew it wouldn't work."

(b) Making Believe: "I wonder what it feels like to be slim and attractive. Like so-and-so. I'm going to imagine I'm like him/her. Yes, just like that. That feels great. I feel self-confident, full of energy and health. I stand and walk as if I've got a great body. I wear nice clothes. I exercise. I eat sensibly. Would so-and-so gorge on chocolate cake? Today, I'm playing the role of a slim person. I act just like a slim person."

When we try to believe, we are brought up short by external reality, which dissipates the desired belief. When we make believe, it doesn't matter what happens, because, after all, we're "only pretending."

Don't be misled by thinking, "It's no good trying to act cheerful if it's not real." Once you start playing a role with emotion and enthusiasm, your body acts *as if* it belongs to another personality for the period of the role-play. It produces immediate physiological changes, even at very deep levels. In chapter 4, we will see that actors can dramatically change their immune systems after 30 minutes, according to the type of role they play.

When did I first realize the power of this idea? With a life-long experience in acting, I had already been using role-playing, almost unconsciously, to achieve certain things in my life. It first really dawned on me what a powerful therapeutic tool it could be, seven years ago in a hypnotherapy class.

The instructor was telling us about an instant transformation produced in an allergy case. He had had a woman in his class who suffered badly from hay fever. It was the season, and she was exhibiting all the symptoms – coughing, sneezing, sniffling, and red, runny nose. She was getting temporary relief by taking prescribed medication every two hours; the aggravated symptoms would remind her when the two hours were up.

When she sought help, the instructor asked if she could remember a time when she was not allergic, and if so, what it was like. She replied that she could remember quite clearly, even though it was ten years ago. "Good", said the instructor, "because what's happening now is that you are playing the role of a person who suffers from allergies. From this moment on, I want you to play the role of a person who is allergy-free. You can recall what it's like, so you have a point of reference. *Act as if* you have no allergies."

That was it. With no other instructions, the woman started to breathe freely and easily. At the end of the day, she had not taken any more medication, and she was still not exhibiting any of the usual symptoms, nor did she have symptoms the next day, or the day after. From this case, the instructor surmised that perhaps we are all just playing different roles, with more or less conscious awareness.

The story struck a chord in me, as I remembered all my previous experiences in theatre, psychology training and elsewhere, which backed up this idea. Here was a very powerful but astonishingly simple tool, which was being misunderstood and neglected. I could not recall ever reading a book that really explored this concept, but clearly it needed to be brought to people's attention.

As I observed this process at work in many examples around me, I began to feel that I should write a book about it myself. For a few years I did no writing, but the idea continued to simmer in my subconscious.

Then one day I found myself having a long telephone conversation with a friend who was suffering from serious health problems. She also happened to be an expert in goal setting and motivation. I mentioned that I had a book in mind, but hadn't managed to get it off the ground. I started to tell her about the concept, and she got more and more excited. Finally she said, "Lee! If you need motivation for writing, I'll give it to you! I need this book right now! I give myself dozens of affirmations but I have to get over my block. I need to act like a healthy person. Get on and do it!" So I did.

And here it is, a book on how to act out your life, to play the roles of all the people you would like to be, to have a ball, and to grow into your true potential by playing.

To organise it for you, I have divided the book into four parts.

First, "Acting As If" – a resumé of what I discovered spontaneously about Making Believe from my own life experiences – i.e., how playing roles can destroy barriers.

Secondly, "Learning from the Experts" – a look at people who already use Make Believe naturally and/or professionally, and at how they do it.

Thirdly, an examination of the concept of "Multiple Selves" – an exploration of all the different "people" you are already, though you may think you are just one "you." We will look at different tried-and-tested ways of enlarging your personal repertoire, to include wonderful new possibilities you may never have dared consider.

Fourthly, "Just Do It!" – a study of how better to put theory into practice in your own life. Already, each preceding chapter concludes with practical exercises, and in the final chapter we will see a variety of approaches to Make Believe – approaches you can put into action *right now*, in your day-to-day living.

Remember, you are already Making Believe anyway, but not consciously. You are already playing the role of who you think you should be or, even worse, you are pretending to be who others think you are. Who told you, anyway, who the real you is?

Making Believe is far from dishonest. It becomes a conscious choice, made with your own free will, to play the role of the person you could be. You are not who you think you are. Free yourself from your past conditioning and become who you *choose* to be, with Make Believe!

Coleridge once wrote, "Poetry is the willing suspension of disbelief." I invite you to unfetter your creative imagination and to make poetry of your life, by willingly suspending your disbelief. Give yourself permission to Make Believe.

PART I

Acting As If

CHAPTER 2

Acting My Life

Although I was unaware of it, the seeds of this idea – making believe to become more true to your self – were planted many long years ago.

Right now, I live in Europe, giving lectures in self-development and hypnosis, as well as offering private hypnotherapy sessions. At another, earlier stage in my life I was a teacher for the South Australian Education Department, in high schools and in Teachers' College. I was also an actress, singer and dancer, both amateur and professional.

I feel that I've experienced so many different careers, relationships and countries that I'm now looking back over several different lifetimes. The unique combination (or collision!) of the worlds of theatre, education and psychology has helped me to develop an insight into the power of make believe, consciously applied.

From my earliest years, when I got to play Mary in the kindergarten nativity play, I was hooked on the personal power that came from performing – playing someone other than myself in front of an audience who accepted and approved of me. At first, this audience was made up of my school friends or the neighbouring children in our street, whom I always led in games of cops and robbers, cowboys and indians, or re-enactments of the latest movie. Later, dance and drama classes followed, with parts in school plays and child roles in adult amateur theatre. I was discovering the glory of the performing arts – music, song, dance, the spoken word, set design and lighting. It was another world, powerful, magic and exciting. What's more, it was a world where adults not only sanctioned make believe, but elevated it to a respected art form.

Adolescence struck and with it all the angst and confusion of personal identity. The overwhelming sense of personal awareness and shyness was almost painful. Just to cope with everyday life, I felt I needed to play roles known only to myself, in my secret inner life.

As a teenager at high school, I would pretend, "Today I am actually a witch with magical powers,"[1] or, "I have lived for 2000 years, and nobody knows my secret." Although I did not actually act out any changes in behaviour, I would mentally repeat such a phrase, like a mantra, as I walked along the bustling school corridors, and I would immediately feel more poised, confident and reassured. These inner fantasies helped me to bolster my self-esteem; otherwise, I would have felt my awkward adolescent brain and body were not ready to face the adult world.

Although I was inclined to be introverted in class, a well-behaved scholarly type, I surprised my teachers by organising a performance of Act III of Julius Caesar by members of my all-girl class, with myself playing the role of Marc Antony. I gave the funeral oration over Caesar's body with all the unrepressed passion of a mini-Marlon Brando. It never occurred to me to be afraid of speaking in public, or being ridiculed by my peers. After all, it was not ME that people were watching – it was Marc Antony! And Marc Antony, of course, was one of history's most impressive and effective orators.

This event established a bit of a reputation for my public speaking, and I was asked to take part in the inter-high school debating contest. I woke up with a jolt to the difference between real life and acting. I was terrified. Unable to play a make believe character, I had to be me, Lee Pascoe, speaking with my own voice and my own opinions. I would be unprotected, exposed before everybody. I just didn't have the confidence in my real self. Somehow I managed to get through the dreaded event, and acquitted myself honourably, but I suffered all the classic symptoms of stage fright – sweaty palms, shortness of breath, dry mouth and heart palpitations. No more of that, thank you! I decided that in future any public appearances would be in character, someone else's character, where I was safe!

At the time, this seemed like a bad thing. I felt faintly ashamed that I was hiding the real me behind a pretend personality. It seemed dishonest. I had recognised an incredibly powerful psychological technique, but had fallen into the trap of false moral judgment.

Because it took me years to get rid of that uncomfortable feeling, a central purpose of this book is to help you get rid of the discomfort and shame as well.

A big step towards that liberation occurred in my twentieth year, at teachers' college. The end-of-year play, organised by the speech and drama department, was to be a musical comedy. The leads would, of course, have to be singers and dancers, as well as actors. I could dance, but I was no singer. At the auditions, I had decided to try for a non-singing character role (a bit of a come-down from the previous year, when I had played Anne Frank). However, I was asked to read for the female lead. I was fine; it was just what they wanted, and I could, of course, sing, couldn't I? Something clicked inside me and I replied, almost nonchalantly, "Oh, yes." Inside, a frantic struggle was taking place. Was this telling a lie? After all, I was a good actress. Surely I could ACT being a singer? I remembered one of my friends who would amuse us with her comedy turns as an opera singer. Despite the clowning, when she was in full swing she actually had a magnificent voice. I could probably do the same, by playing the role of a musical-comedy star.

The make believe situation won the day. Everyone apparently believed I could sing, I got the part, and the show was a great success. It was "Salad Days", and I had the time of my life, as the song goes. I had developed a new talent, which might have stayed dormant, because I didn't believe in it. (I also conquered the grief of a personal loss by plunging into a joyous, life-affirming experience – but that's another story.)

A subtle shift of consciousness had occurred, and I now accepted that make believe was a liberating, not a hiding, experience. Somehow I had been able to become more my self by playing that extended role. The pretence became real.

Over the next 18 years, the study of speech and drama continued to be an important learning experience for me – not just the skills, but also the continuing sense of discovery of who I really was, and what I could be.

I will pass over the details of these personal discoveries and take a leap forward in time to my departure from Australia. This was a dramatic life change. I was off on an adventure to the other side of the world, with a job lined up to teach English for a year in a Parisian high school for fashion students. I had half time off to study anything I liked – what a golden opportunity! Was it to be philosophy or classical literature at the Sorbonne? No. I jumped at the chance to enrol at the internationally-renowned Jacques Lecoq Mime School, which had inspired several of my colleagues in Australian theatre.

The school was a glorious hodge-podge of languages, cultures and ages, with more foreign students than native French. But since we were learning mime, the universal language, even students with rudimentary French were soon able to plunge into the activities.

I could probably write a book about my year at Lecoq. I don't think any of us came away the same person. However, two experiences stand out especially, both of which have relevance to playing a make believe role.

The first was the concept of the neutral mask. We were all accustomed to the phenomenon that occurs when an actor puts on a mask. He/she immediately adopts the stance, gestures, mood and voice of the mask's character. Children also do this quite naturally – they become the character whose face or head they are wearing. The neutral mask, however, was radically different. It was a plain oval shape with slits or holes for the eyes, nose and mouth, but no other features. The face had absolutely no expression – it was ageless, sexless and emotionless.

At the improvisation exercise where the mask was introduced, the first student actor to put it on froze in panic in front of his audience of comrades. He had no idea what he was supposed to do. How do you act being nobody or nothing? In turn, we each experienced the same sensation – we felt exposed, naked, unprotected. Whereas normally you could hide your identity behind the mask's personality, now there was, literally, nothing to hide behind... not even your own face! The act of putting on a mask, in fact, removed the mask we were already wearing. It was quite a psychological shock to discover that we were each so identified with our particular role, or persona.[2] Now this persona was revealed to be arbitrary, and subject to change.

Through a gradual, painful process, the body wearing the mask learnt to rid itself of all the exterior mannerisms that had become the habitual self. We were discovering the neutral centre, being stripped down to that essential nature common to all humanity, to which the actor must return before he can grow outwards and express himself in a myriad of different roles. Having been confronted with the fact that each of us was already playing a role, totally unconsciously, we now had to remove that role in order to explore new ones, with full awareness.

The next illuminating episode occurred over two weeks of class. Our assignment was to choose a role – a character as diametrically opposed to our selves as we could imagine – and to adopt this role completely during class time. While we were present at the school, during movement, acrobatic and improvisation class, even traveling to and from school, we were to do everything in character. We were to act as if we had actually become this invented person; we were to move and speak as this person, wear the clothes, hairstyle and (if appropriate) makeup of this person, react emotionally and defend the beliefs of this person.

To my chosen role I gave the name of Barbara. (I realised later that some significant Barbaras in my life had been apparently superior beings to whom I had lost out.) My Barbara was a Greta Garbo type, mysterious, aloof, sophisticated, self-assured, confident of her innate superiority, unprepared to suffer fools lightly – all the things that, in my naïveté, I believed I was not. I swept my hair back, wore my most glamorous outfits and high heels (totally impractical for class), and constantly touched up my immaculate makeup. I felt really cool being Barbara! The best part was when I had a confrontation with a particularly sarcastic male teacher. Without any of my normal confusion or hesitation, I calmly put him in his place, much to his amazement – and to my own! I exulted in this new-found power. Around me, other students were also plunging into their roles, playing them to the hilt, thoroughly enjoying not being themselves.

After a week, it was becoming hard to keep up the persona. Perhaps because we had chosen hastily, perhaps because it was so foreign. At any rate, the next surprise came along: now we were to reverse roles! Against everything our role repressed, we now had to create a new character, totally the opposite. It was a stretched elastic band being released. The tension of playing one extreme rebounded to the other. Overnight I became a bumptious tomboy, careless, casual, matey and arrogant. A typical Australian "ocker" type. "G'day, mate, 'ow ya goin'? No worries!" I wore shorts and sneakers, no makeup, my hair stuck up in spikes. I was loud, vulgar and boisterous, and how I enjoyed it! It was such a relief after all that isolated self-control. I felt as if I had fallen right through my normal personality and out on the other side!

In time, this character, too, lost its initial attraction, and the same thing seemed to be happening with my classmates.

A week later, we all returned to being ourselves, and behaving normally, realising that this, too, was probably just a role, which seemed real because we had practiced it till it became habitual. In retrospect, I enjoyed being both these other people. It was an opportunity to explore fully some parts of myself which I would never normally *dare* to express. I was able to discover and keep bits I liked, integrating them into myself, or keeping them in reserve for special occasions.

What a shame this life-enhancing experience was only available to actors-in-training. The whole game did not require professional acting skills – merely a lively imagination. If only this sort of experience could be available to the general public. I wanted to tell as many people as possible about how they, too, could discover and break through their limits!

The whole exercise provoked some very profound questions:

… Who are we really?

… Who *decides* who we are?

… Where do we find our roles?

… To what extent do others impose roles upon us until we believe them to be ourselves?

Maybe there is no limit to who we can be, when we exercise conscious choice!

Exercises

Exercise: FINDING YOUR VOICE

In your car, or in some place where you can sing your heart out without fear of being heard, try out different voices, such as singing as your favourite pop stars or opera singers. Imagine you are Pavarotti or Callas, Elvis or Madonna, Bob Dylan or Janis Joplin, Paul Robeson or Ella Fitzgerald. Experiment with male and female, high and low, modern and classical. Have fun! No one is around to criticise or make fun of you. You may even discover that you have a magnificent voice or, at the very least, that you actually enjoy singing.

A secondary advantage is that this will help reduce stress. If you're stuck in a traffic jam, instead of building up tension and damaging your immune system – sing!

Research on brain imaging shows that singing controls the amount of brain activity and slows neural impulses. Singing also helps calm your breathing and heart rate to a normal pace.[3]

Exercise: PLAY A NEW ROLE

When you go on holiday, or join a new club, somewhere where nobody knows you and you are a completely unknown factor, invent a new persona and play it to the hilt. (Some people do this anyway, becoming completely different personalities in their leisure activities than they are at home or at work.) Do things and say things that you would never normally do, because your family and friends would know it's not you. Have fun, invent, explore, discover. No one needs to know you're only pretending.

PART II

Learning from the Experts

Introduction

Until now, you may well have considered that make believe was only an escape or a fantasy. Now, perhaps, you are beginning to understand that it is also an extraordinary and powerful tool for self-improvement.

To use this tool takes skill, which needs to be learned and honed like any other skill. But where can this skill be studied and how can it be practiced? The next three chapters will show you how the technique of Make Believe is *already* used by three different groups of people – children, actors and hypnotists.

In their own way, each of these groups specialises in make believe and has developed its own rituals, attitudes and techniques to put make believe into practice as efficiently as possible. Where better to learn this skill, maligned and unrecognised by the general public, than from these experts? So, sit back and let me introduce you to the best pretenders in the business.

We will be starting with those experts that we ourselves once were when we, too, were still young: children.

Childhood

"Let's pretend." How do these words make you feel?

For most of us, they immediately conjure up our childhood, and with it a wonderful sense of freedom and fun. "Let's pretend" were magic words which transported us to other dimensions, beyond reality, where we could be anyone and anything we wanted to be.

When we were children, all the games we played were experiments for real life. Our notion of self was not yet fixed, but constantly fluid and changing. We changed roles constantly, with a sense of delight and adventure, because in our game playing we could be, temporarily, anyone we chose. We were surrounded by role models, not only those that society offered us, but all the characters who presented themselves to us in fairy stories, films, novels. Everything was grist to the mill of our imagination: "What shall I play at today?" "Who shall I be today?"

Make believe gave us the freedom to test qualities in ourselves we would never have permitted if we had already a frozen notion of this *is* me, that's *not* me. We could try out amazing courage, confidence, intelligence, joy, ferocity, terror, triumph – as easily as slipping on another change of clothes.

An infinite variety of possibilities was available. It never occurred to us to be distracted from the experience by thinking, "But it's not *real*." Sure, we knew that. But because we were just imagining, we could give the experience our total concentration and involvement.

What a terrible loss if now, as an adult, you were to deny yourself this freedom, because you felt too mature for such childish nonsense!

THE BEST EDUCATION

Make Believe – pretending, imitating, playing out roles – is the child's school of life. It is how he learns and this learning is as natural and easy for him as breathing. It is how he develops into maturity, both physically and mentally. Piaget posited his steps in child development by observing children at play and noting how they reached new concepts in abstract thinking through physical playing.[1] Every child is a mini-laboratory, testing and experimenting – through playing.

Dr. Carla Hannaford, educational kinesiologist, says in her book *Smart Moves* that "playing lays down new neuronal pathways and creates new structures for learning to take place."[2] She describes how a child of two to three years will not only imitate the adults around him, but will even take up a body position to mimic a newly discovered object – an effort to understand it in a corporeal way. In other words, to learn about the object and to integrate it into his world experience, he will *pretend to be* that object.

It seems this imitative behaviour is innate, part of our basic psychological make-up. Neurologists have recently discovered the presence in the brain of "mirror molecules."[3] Certain motor areas of the brain light up, under scanners, when we watch another person performing an action. This represents a mental process whereby we are already imagining ourselves in the same position, performing the same actions. This in turn leads to an urge to actually repeat the behaviour ourselves. Such imitation is fundamental to all human learning, a natural, inborn impulse. We try it out ourselves – if not physically, then in our imagination.

So, when a child at play announces, "I'm the teacher – you're the class!" or, "I'm Daddy and you're Mummy," he is following the impulse of his mirror molecules. He is trying to grasp, through experimenting in play, the concepts of different personalities, social structures, authority and power, emotional relationships and conflict – all those highly sophisticated concepts that are necessary for existing in our society. The child is, literally, *learning by pretending*. Far from just playing a game, he is rehearsing for real life.

Child psychologists tell us that a newborn baby has no sense of separate identity from his mother or from the world around him.

He spends the first part of his life discovering what is me and what is not me. At first, this takes place through sensory impressions: he looks at, crawls toward, touches and tastes everything possible in his environment. Later, he moves into the stage of pretending to be the outside object or person, as Dr. Hannaford describes, by mimicking its qualities with his own body. Again, he is discovering the answer to the question, "Is this me or not me? Little by little, he is building up his concept of self, his sense of personal identity.

This process can continue as a lifelong experience, so long as we do not allow our sense of self to rigidify as an adult. Too often, at maturity we have developed a fixed concept of who we are, and we will dismiss any further role-learning experiences as, "That's not me!" As long as we keep the playful, open mind of a child, we can go on discovering new and exciting elements of who we can be and what we can do – as long as we dare go on pretending.

PRETEND THERAPY

When, for some reason, children are unable to develop their capacity to play "Let's pretend," they may suffer severe deficiencies in their developmental growth. Adults – parents, educators, or therapists – may need to step in and gently guide them in this direction. For example, Strategic Family Therapy (Jay Haley and Chloe Madanes) uses metaphors and the therapy of "Pretend" as a large part of their system. Parenting.com runs classes to help parents "nurture the power of Make Believe. . . . Talking to stuffed animals, playing house and creating cities out of blocks may seem like mere play, but these activities develop imagination and the skills kids will need for grown-up success."

Boris Cyrulnik, French psychiatrist and writer,[4] has always insisted upon the importance of children's make believe as a preparation for adulthood.

"All children play "let's pretend". A child who cannot play at pretending is worrying, and clearly has serious difficulties with relationships. He dare not, and cannot, manipulate the mental world of other people. So he is unable to create the subjective relationship that characterises the human condition. Before the development of speech, from 15 months of age, the child has to know how to pretend to cry or to hide himself. It's a sign of his skill in subjective relationships. Making up myths is a necessary part of our way of identifying ourselves. "When I grow up, I'll be Tarzan," or, "I'll have a house with ten children" are internal myths that empower identity: "I dream, therefore I will be." It is vital for the structuring of self... A child who does not dream of his future is condemned to live in the immediate present, and thus cannot realise his desires. Woe to those who have never pretended; they are prisoners of reality."[5]

So, according to this highly respected psychiatrist, not only is pretending necessary for our psychological health; it is actually unhealthy if one's entire identity is wholly invested in playing out one single role, real or imaginary!

One of my American colleagues, Susan Fox, is a therapist who uses puppet shows in her work with children. She often creates a little play based on a particular family problem and demonstrates with the puppet characters how to overcome it, sometimes using quite complex skills (assertiveness, self-confidence, respect for others' needs). Children shriek with laughter but become wide-eyed with wonder and recognition as they identify with the character that triumphs over adversity. They are already vicariously pretending to be the central character.

STORIES

All children (and many child-like adults!) love stories – fairy stories, legends, fables, plays and novels. The incredible success of Harry Potter suggests that the modern child, apparently so sophisticated and technologically informed, is just as passionate for a good story as his predecessors over the centuries. And a story gives just as much opportunity for make believe as active play.

The perennial favourites are those that allow the child to identify with the hero or heroine. In imagination, the child becomes the brave young boy who must kill the dragon, the beautiful princess who must be rescued from the ogre, the youngest son or daughter who must overcome poverty and oppression with their goodness, honesty and courage. This identification can be at a completely subconscious level.[6] There is no need to say to a child, "Pretend that you are the young prince/princess;" the process of identifying oneself with the protagonist is automatic and immediate: "I'm like that!" or, "I could be like that!"

This is why Harry Potter is so popular. He has provided for millions of children of different languages and cultures, the chance to introduce some magic into this modern, technological age. Oppressed, poor, an orphan, he suddenly discovers he is a Very Important Person in the wizard world. However, Harry must still prove himself by demonstrating all the classic virtues of the old fairy stories: courage, perseverance, discipline, honesty and loyalty to his friends. All this while remaining the boy next door, with typical hatred of homework, arguments with friends, confusion and fear when faced with things greater than he can understand.

In the 21st century, children need more than ever to rehearse for reality in the richness of their imagination.

You, too, now you are grown up, are still identifying with the characters in films and novels, but you probably dismiss the idea immediately as unrealistic, and shelve the whole experience as an escapist fantasy. You can learn a lot by becoming as a child again. If you try the exercise YOU'RE THE STAR at the end of this chapter, you'll be delighted with the results.

LET'S HAVE FUN!

When you think of your own childhood and your favourite games, do you remember how you *felt*? Do you remember the sense of light-heartedness and enthusiasm that accompanied your actions? You could apply yourself to a game of Let's Pretend with a concentration and a single-mindedness that would serve you well even today, but without the competitiveness, stress and sense of responsibility that pervade adult life.

No, I do not believe we should try to bring back the misnamed "best years of our life," but I firmly believe we need to recapture that particular creative energy and freedom that we associate with having fun. Do you remember being robbed of this energy over the years with such remarks as "This isn't a game!" "This is important!" "Can't you stop fooling around and take things seriously?" School lessons and parents drummed into us the importance of effort, discipline and gravity, and we were told it was for our own good!

Unfortunately, this grown up attitude robs us not only of our *joie de vivre*, but also of our efficiency. The stress of making an effort has a stultifying, restricting effect on our energy and concentration. In educational kinesiology, research has shown that a child is physically weakened when he is told, "Try!" or "Make an Effort!" At the same time his mental functioning is affected, there being less flow in the connections between the two brain hemispheres. In demonstrations of hypnotic suggestion, where the aim is to make an action difficult or impossible, the instruction is, "Try...but you can't! Try harder! It's impossible!" To facilitate the same action, the instruction is simply, "Stop trying." The subject then relaxes and easily performs the desired action.

So, what we can learn from children is that keeping a sense of fun and enjoying our activities is not incompatible with being efficient and getting things done. On the contrary, an inflated sense of the importance and seriousness of a job can interfere with its accomplishment. The stress of "getting it right" can actually block us. "Let's just pretend for a while" removes immediately the heavy weight of responsibility and frees us up.

When, as one of the eldest students in the Jacques LeCoq Mime School, I had to take part in acrobatic classes, I kept freezing up. The perfectionist part of me insisted that I get this right – it was important! There I was, one memorable day, standing in line to do a forward somersault... in the air! We had to run towards the instructor's outstretched arm, and at a precise moment and distance, leap into the air and dive forward into a roll. He would then assist us by flipping us over to land upright. I had never done anything like this in my life before. As my turn arrived and the instructor turned to me, he saw the look of anguish frozen on my face. He smiled and called gently, "Lee, just play the fool!" ("Lee, un peu de folie!")

That was all I needed. Why not? I could just pretend this was huge fun. I charged forward, shut my eyes, dived into the air and... a rush of air, the room span and then bingo! I was on my feet! I couldn't believe it! What a sense of triumph, of liberation! As I rejoined the group to sounds of applause, I grinned to myself. It was easy. After all, it was 'just child's play!'

Exercises

Exercise: WAKE UP WITH ANTICIPATION

Do you wake with a sense of dread at all the responsibilities that face you in the day ahead? Remember how you woke up as a child, with a sense of wonder and excitement at all the possibilities that lay waiting?

Next morning, as you first drift into waking consciousness, say to yourself, "What will I play today?" Imagine you are *pretending* to be... a secretary, a clerk, an executive, a teacher, a mother. What fun!

Plan the day as if you are preparing for a highly complex and amusing game. If you really can't find anything at all that you can look forward to, perhaps it is time to re-structure your life. You may have lost your way.

"When I grow up, I want to be..." You *are* grown up. Keep *wanting* to be.

Exercise: YOU'RE THE STAR!

Next time you see a film that you enjoy, allow yourself the luxury of make believe that you did as a child. While watching, let yourself identify consciously with the main protagonist. Ask yourself, how would I feel if I were feeling that/doing that/experiencing that? Afterwards, in a comfortable armchair or in your bed, close your eyes and daydream what it would be like being this person. First, imagine yourself playing the role, doing the same things and living the same events as in the film. Then, transpose this character to your own life. See yourself in this role, confronting the situations you meet every day. Borrow their personality temporarily. How do you react now? Do you enjoy this? If it doesn't quite fit, are there any specific traits you would like to keep and adapt to your own personal and professional life?

In Make Believe, you can be anyone you want to be. Thus, in reality, you can be more richly *you.*

CHAPTER 4

The Theatre

All the world's a stage,
And all the men and women merely players;
They have their exits and their entrances,
And one man in his time plays many parts.

William Shakespeare, *As You Like It, II, 7*

Shakespeare was himself an actor as well as a playwright and understood the importance of playing a role well. He also saw the theatre as a metaphor for life; the roles played being not only the different ages of man, but also all the different personalities with which we express ourselves, consciously or unconsciously.

An actor on stage is, in fact, just pretending, but no audience would ever consider using such demeaning terminology. Actors are seen as exercising a highly cultivated and well-respected art, which they have learned and developed over the years, honing their skills with each part. This is their profession, and we would do well to see how we could learn from their expertise.

This includes those of you who have never been in a play, or even seen one live in a theatre. You are, in fact, already an actor in the play of your own life, as the Bard so aptly puts it. As such, you can become a far more effective, and conscious, player, from observing how professional actors learn to be *not themselves*.

This chapter shows how these obvious experts of Make Believe think, train and behave. I will be drawing parallels with your own role-playing in daily life and creating exercises you can put into practice right away for yourself.

The actor's craft involves being able to identify with, inhabit and interpret a character, investing all his physical, mental and emotional energies for the period of the performance, and then being able to withdraw from that character almost instantaneously, to switch to another character or to take a curtain call.

Being unable to step in and out of a role on demand is seen as a lack of skill, except by the more extreme Method actors of the sixties, who seemed to forget that it was all, however elaborate and sophisticated, a big game of make believe.

One anecdote from Hollywood relates how, in one scene in "Marathon Man," Dustin Hoffman's character is meant to be exhausted from several days' adventures without sleep. Unable to simply pretend that he was in a bad state, Hoffman, a Method actor, actually stayed up all night so that his exhaustion would be real and he could become his character. His co-actor, Laurence Olivier, gave him a withering look and commented, "My dear boy, why don't you try acting?"

This is the type of actor who, having immersed himself completely in the role of king, hero or villain, must now take his curtain call, and no longer knows what role to play. Once he has stopped pretending to be someone else, he does not know who to play before the audience, and may actually shrink in embarrassment. The great opera singers, for example, never have this problem. They take their call in the role of Diva, resplendent in the glory of playing the great Star, which, after all, is just another role that they have rehearsed to perfection.

Those actors who have not forgotten their humble beginnings can still remember that initial hope, often expressed by students while still adolescents, who when asked why they want to be in theatre, will reply: "Because I want to be someone else." [1]

Is that a weakness or a strength? It depends on your point of view. The essence of my argument is that, unless playing a role becomes a cowardly escape from reality, it is a huge strength – one of the most powerful tools for self-discovery that exist.

Most personal development programmes will tell you that what hinders you from expressing your real potential is blocks, or limiting belief systems. How to overcome them? Not by hoping they will go away, not by using them as an excuse, not by denying their existence and not by opposing them with an effort of will. Simply by pretending that you are someone else, who does not have these blocks!

FREEDOM TO BE

An actor is given free rein to go beyond all the limits imposed by his culture, his education, his genetic inheritance, his physical build, his race, even his (or her) sex, to explore every possible type of existence known to man or written by playwright. He is not, of course, completely free, as he cannot always choose the roles allotted him. This is, after all, a job and not a therapy.[2] This is why some actors prefer to remain amateurs, when they can choose their roles without the constraints of having to earn a living.

Actors who find themselves repeating the same role year in and year out become frustrated and discontented. Unknowns who become big stars playing a certain character in a TV soap will, after only a few years, give up the fame and fortune to break out on their own. Their publicity agent announces they do not want to be typecast. They do not want to be the same person for the rest of their lives.

How much more true is that statement, for a role we have to play 24 hours a day, 365 days a year? Do *we* really want to be the same persons for the rest of our lives?

THAT WASN'T ME

Even those of us who have never set foot on a stage have felt this urge to be free from the fetters of self – that person we, and others, perceive ourselves to be. How liberating it would be to play the clown, for example, instead of keeping up the image of seriousness and respectability. And because of cultural restrictions, we may have to get drunk at a party to express that part of us. At the time, we may feel wonderfully uninhibited, intoxicated with freedom as much as with alcohol. However, next morning, back in our regular role, we are embarrassed and sheepishly excuse ourselves: "I don't know what came over me." But who is *what* and who is *me*? And how can we say which one is *real*?

An actor has the perfect excuse for *not* being himself. He is *in character* when he fools around, explodes with rage, or collapses in despair. Those of us who are not permitted this luxury may find ourselves distressed by such uncontrolled outbursts. "That wasn't me," we will apologise. If it wasn't you, who was it? Someone else pretending to be you... or you pretending to be someone else?

"That wasn't me," can also, too often, be an excuse for being less than we are, for not admitting our inner strength, wisdom or beauty.

Many years ago, I was teaching voice to a class of amateur theatre enthusiasts. They had learned how tension and bad habits caused most people to seize up their throats when they wanted to increase vocal power. They were going through a series of breathing and movement exercises to release the sound from the level of their diaphragm muscles. One small, mousey woman in particular was straining dreadfully to produce a little squeaking sound. To encourage them, I said, "Squat down in a martial arts position and *pretend* you're a fierce Samurai warrior. Now, give me a mighty warrior roar from the diaphragm. Scare me!"

Suddenly a powerful "Hah-h-h!" bellowed out from the vicinity of the mouse-woman. We all turned towards her in amazement. She, also, turned to look around her, in bewilderment, as if wondering where that formidable voice had come from. Then, completely mortified, she spluttered, "That wasn't ME!" Not only was she afraid to recognise her own power, she felt compelled to deny it when confronted with it.

This is a perfect example of the liberating effect of Make Believe. If what she had been doing was false pretence, she could never have produced that awe-inspiring sound. But in this case, the pretence was true in that it allowed her REAL power to be released. What was false, in fact, was the timid little persona that she had been conditioned into believing was her true self.

The story has a happy ending. This same woman went on to take a starring role in a later production, impressing even professional actors with her ease and confidence. Even more important, this same ease and confidence she displayed on stage became a natural part of her daily life. Her family and friends were amazed and delighted by the transformation.

BECOMING THE PART

"But isn't there a danger" you may say, "in actually believing you become another person! What happens if you forget you are playing a role?"

Here, too, we can learn from how professional actors cope with this paradox. How much does an actor actually *become* his role? Does he forget himself, or does he remain aware that he is acting/pretending? It seems that both are true at the same time – a psychological paradox. On the one hand, a really good actor will lose himself in his part, feeling real anguish, joy, rage – to the extent of producing all the real physical symptoms, crying real tears, trembling, blushing or turning ashen, even, as we will see in a moment, changing the chemical makeup of his blood stream.

Shakespeare observed this phenomenon in Hamlet:

Is it not monstrous that this player here,
But in a fiction, in a dream of passion,
Could force his soul so to his own conceit
That from her working all his visage wann'd,
Tears in his eyes, distraction in's aspect,
A broken voice, and his whole function suiting
With forms to his conceit? and all for nothing!
For Hecuba!
What's Hecuba to him, or he to Hecuba,
That he should weep for her?

Hamlet, *Act II, sc.2.*

Yet, on the other hand, he must remain completely aware of all his actions from the point of view of an outside observer. He has to remember his lines, wait for the correct cues, time his moves to the dialogue, manipulate props – all those mechanical things which must be taken care of so the show runs smoothly. If another actor is late for an entrance or misses a cue, he must have his wits about him to ad-lib. If there is a technical problem, he must cover up for it while remaining in character.

One of my hypnosis students in Paris is a well-known and respected opera singer. Having just been the demonstration subject for a particularly moving regression, in which he "relived" a drowning sequence, he was asked by the class how he felt during the experience. Had he actually believed he was drowning and forgotten all about the present existence?

"Not at all," he explained. "At the same time it was totally real, and yet part of me was aware I was sitting here next to Lee, describing the whole event."

His face lit up as he recognised the connection to his theatrical life. "It was like when I'm on stage. I can be totally wrapped up in playing Don José – I am consumed by passion, jealousy, sorrow – I *am* Don José! It's real for me. But when the moment comes to stab Carmen I am perfectly aware I must make a feint and turn the knife aside so I won't harm the actress."

My mind flashed back to when our theatre group was being trained for a fight sequence by a stunt man. He'd once had to protect himself from a Hamlet who started frothing at the mouth and slashing at him – and who finished up in a mental asylum! "The more you keep your cool, the more you can express emotion," he explained. "If it's too real, if you get too involved, it's no longer believable to the audience. Keep the control, remember you're pretending."

So there's your answer. Pretend for all you're worth, but remember you're pretending.

Of course, we all *know* theatre is make believe, but we're willing to suspend our disbelief – as an audience and as a performer. Then it can be elevated to such glorious artistic heights that it becomes sheer magic – that knife-edge balance between reality and pretence that makes an audience hold its breath and which, for the actor, becomes an almost mystical peak experience, where time stands still and he can do nothing which is not in perfect harmony.

This experience is known in other areas, like sports performance, as the "flow" state.[3] When you teach yourself to achieve this balance, both acting out your life, while directing and observing it, you too can attain the state of flow, or harmony, in your daily existence.

PHYSICAL REACTIONS

The power of making believe can produce very real physical effects in the human body. In an experiment in Immune System Reactivity,[4] Nicolas R. S. Hall, PhD, had already worked with cases of Multiple Personality Disorder (a recognised mental illness first described in the MSDIII), when he first thought of studying professional actors. He had seen seemingly impossible physiological changes taking place in just a few seconds of changing personality – "switching".[5] He had also noticed that, although the personality changes were of a genuinely pathological nature, they were sometimes enhanced or exaggerated on the part of the female patient, which gave rise to the question, "Was she acting?"

When this particular avenue was no longer available, he turned his attention to the closest possible situation in a non-pathological setting. He studied professional actors in a controlled environment. You could say actors are constantly producing multiple personalities. "Many actors would agree that assuming a dramatic role could seem like a multiple personality experience."

The study was conducted at Arizona State University. Two dual-character short plays were selected – one a comedy, "Lucy Does a TV Commercial," the other a serious play whose main tone was depression.

The plays were presented at the same time of day before a live audience over a two-week period, and each day saw a reversed sequence; e.g. Monday: comedy, then drama; Tuesday: drama, then comedy. A blood sample was taken at the beginning and end of each performance. The results showed clear changes in the blood immune system.

"The data suggested that there was a correlation between the type of personality being performed and immune responsiveness." The female performer especially, whose role passed from joyful madcap (The "I Love Lucy" character) to tragic, repressed victim "exhibited an elevated rate of T- and B- lymphocyte cell division after the comedy, and a decrease after the drama. The same pattern was reflected in the production of inter-leukin 2 ...

"The male performer exhibited comparable changes consistent with the personality being performed. For him, (since his character still maintained a sense of control in the drama), it was performing the anxious, uptight role associated with the comedy that resulted in the larger decrease in the immune system measures."

These are actually very encouraging results. To effect positive (or negative) physical changes, a psychologically normal person can use acting skills. It seems we can *choose* to play good or bad health!

Right now, as you are reading this book, stop and become aware of your physical posture and energy. Have you slipped into the role of being tired or lacking in energy? Take a moment to act as if you are in radiant good health. Your immune system and your whole body will receive the message and start working to produce a positive outcome.

ACTING AS THERAPY

The results of his experiments suggested to Hall that "acting might be useful as a medical intervention. For example, is it possible to take a person with a classic C-type personality – a very passive individual, a person who has a difficult time expressing anger – and by teaching acting techniques bring out a more aggressive, take-charge type of personality – one that would lift the person out of the mode of feeling helpless and hopeless? In turn, could that be reflected in a better prognosis for dealing with the person's disease?"

In fact, several different disciplines are already using acting classes, neither as a leisure activity nor as skill training, but as personal therapy or improvement.

Psycho-drama (see chapter 7) is a whole system of playing out the different roles in conflicted family and social relationships.

Numerous courses exist which offer acting workshops for self-understanding and discovery. Just recently in my post box I received this:

"All the World's a Stage." In this workshop you use acting, costumes and some radical role-playing exercises to help you become *more of who you really are*. And you will gain a new sensitivity to what makes others act the way they do and a unique understanding of the hidden dynamic that operates between human beings in all social settings."

As well as self-understanding, we can also develop our understanding, tolerance and compassion for people we would normally consider totally different from ourselves. If we are to play that character, we must find something in ourselves that resonates with that person, even if he is a murderer or terrorist. In my own experience, I've played aristocrat and beggar, genius and deranged, nun and prostitute, tragedy queen and court jester. How could I be anti-Semitic, for example, when I've suffered the terror of being discovered playing Anne Frank, or celebrated Hanukkah in "Fiddler on the Roof"?

Acting is the ultimate form of putting yourself in someone else's shoes to develop empathy. The very word "compassion" means "feeling with". While playing the role, we share in the character's emotions.

Pretending to be a whole range of different people has helped me both to expand my own possibilities and to connect with the essential humanity that lies within us all.

You will find a multitude of other self-help classes that use acting as their chief working tool. Just look in your local adult education programme, or the small ads section of the health and psychology magazines.

One approach, which dates from the 1960's, is described in the book, *The Master Game*, (Robert S. de Ropp, 1968). In chapter V, entitled "The Theatre of the Selves" he talks of how each of us has a multiplicity of selves, and must learn to "regard all the manifestations of his being as objectively as if they were part of a theatrical experience... The 'I's' or selves change like characters on a stage and each 'I' suffers from the delusion that it has a will of its own." He compares these selves to a box of clockwork dolls, with different costumes and behaviour patterns, having no free will, but wound up and activated by circumstances.

De Ropp proposes two methods of transcending this level of existence. First, Inner Theatre, is an internal mental creation, where one practices "projecting the self in its various aspects and watching its behaviour as if it were somebody else." From outside of the theatre one observes the different roles, becoming aware that this is all pretence, on a mechanical level. Only by recognising this, can one learn to escape mechanical reaction and exercise conscious choice. This mental work must also be linked to the practice of Outer Theatre, in which the student attempts, in his everyday life, to play some role that is slightly different from his habitual ones.

Many people are, in a sense, attempting to use this technique, explains de Ropp, when they make a resolution to change their behaviour patterns. "A person who habitually loses his temper resolves to 'play it cool' – a timid person resolves to 'play it strong' – a lazy person resolves an active role, etc." The resolutions are usually broken because the person remains stuck in the habitual limited repertoire of gestures and facial expressions that determine his role.

However, the student who consciously uses Outer Theatre as a technique has a different aim – to gain self-knowledge. To understand and to extend the limitations of his roles, he practices *internal manifestations*, creating situations that deliberately place him in a position where he must play a role not in his natural repertoire. The very fact that he may feel uncomfortable doing something different is a step toward self-awareness. He learns to be more aware of what he is doing and how he is doing it, thus developing the muscle of his free will. He becomes inner-directed rather than directed by external stimuli. The chapter concludes with an apt simile from Epictetus, who "compared the Stoic philosopher to a 'spy of God', capable of adopting all sorts of disguises, beggar or king, slave or free, but always inwardly independent of the role he happened to be playing."

We may seem to have moved a long way from acting techniques to discovering higher consciousness. However, this element has always been present in theatre, since prehistoric times. By acting out different roles, man has strived to answer the eternal questions, "Who am I? Who could I be?"

THEATRE AS SPIRITUAL CENTRE

In antiquity, there was no division, as there is today, between science, art and religion. All of these activities were bound together. An action might have a practical purpose, involving a certain knowledge and technical skill, but be carried out with an awareness of rhythm, harmony and pattern, and an overall concept of its spiritual influence, connecting man with the gods.

So, for example, as preparation for the act of hunting, man would go through an elaborate ritual of music and dance, acting out the roles of the animal hunted, as well as the hunter. In a spiritual dimension, this gave him control over elements of nature, which were otherwise uncontrolled forces. This was the whole basis of magic and religion. The shaman was both priest and actor, who by pretending to be the triumphant hunter and/or the slain animal, used the law of correspondence – that is, imitating in gesture and ritual what he wished to produce in tribal life. By representing this in the appropriate ritual, he considered he was able to imbue himself with the forces of nature and gain some control over them. For primitive man, this was a matter of survival, in an existence where he would otherwise have felt helpless, at the mercy of incomprehensible powers that he ascribed to spirits or gods.

This link continued to develop as man's life became more complex and civilised. The ancient rituals of Egypt, Mesopotamia, Greece and Rome continued to involve humans acting out the roles of gods, powers and kings, thereby establishing a connection with the Divine. By the end of the Middle Ages, the church began actually excommunicating actors, seeing in them a dangerous rival to its own church ritual for the attention of the populace.

Certain pockets of hidden knowledge, however, including the Sufis, continued to operate as mystery schools, handing down the old traditions of actor as priest, priest as actor.

In our own secular age, religion is rarely considered an essential part of life. It seems to have lost its practical purpose as a source of help in daily activities, as well as its power to uplift and illuminate. But the people still feel, even unconsciously, a need to connect with the profound secrets of life. Man has a longing for the sacred, which, if he cannot find in the church, he will seek elsewhere, even if he does not understand what he is looking for. Deep down, he needs to unite with something larger than himself.

For many, this can still be found in the theatre, which provides the door to another reality. All sorts of magical possibilities are offered which are normally denied to the soul starving in a material, competitive existence.

It is not surprising that I learnt some of my most powerful lessons in life in drama schools or in rehearsals. During my year at the Lecoq School, for example, it gradually dawned on me that what we were doing was much more than learning the skills of a trade. I had the distinct impression that we were in an ancient mystery school. We were discovering profound truths, not by indoctrination, but by challenge, exploration and personal discovery – a whole series of "aha" experiences. We were not learning to "fake it" – we were learning to peel away all the outside layers of onion to get closer to the essential truth.

We do not all, of course, have to be actors-in-training to experience this. Just being in the audience of a theatre can produce that wonderful feeling of being uplifted beyond the self. The theatre becomes as a church, and I do not mean this in any sacrilegious sense – in fact, the contrary. What lifts and inspires us is the possibility to explore, *vicariously*, every dimension of life – the high and the low, the tragic and the comic, the sacred and the profane. Musical comedy and vaudeville have their place as much as opera and the classics. By identifying with the actor, we become what he becomes; we experience what he experiences for us. Just temporarily, we become *more* than what we are.

The moment when, as an audience member, we not only resonate with the character, but also understand that we possess within us the possibility to be like him, is a moment of self-realisation. If free will is the essence of humanity, it is in the theatre that each of us can realise, at an essential level of being, "I can *choose* my role."

Exercises

Exercise: JOIN A GROUP

Join a drama class, or an amateur theatre group even if you've never done anything like it before. Join even if your incredibly busy life allows it just for a short time. Apart from full scope for make believe, for all sorts of different characters, you will be in an environment that takes role-playing very seriously, and will encourage you to develop it fully with the support of fellow actors, costumes, scenery and props.

You will be surprised and delighted to find what unsuspected talents you possess. You may find you have more confidence, sensitivity, intuition, energy and enthusiasm than you believed.

And whatever you do, don't allow yourself to become typecast. The whole idea is to develop a range of roles from which you can consciously *choose*.

Exercise: RE-INVENT YOURSELF

Study how celebrities who wish to stay at the top of their profession continually re-invent themselves. David Bowie and Madonna are two examples. Just when the public thinks it knows who they are and what to expect of them, they change roles!

Look at your own life – with family, with friend, with colleagues. Do they know who you are? Have they come to expect always the same things from you? Re-invent yourself!

At first, just do one thing that's different, as De Ropp recommends in his Outer Theatre Technique.

Wear something you would not normally wear. Go somewhere you would not normally go. Strike up a conversation with someone you would not normally speak to. If you find yourself thinking, "This isn't me!" recognise that this is your conventional image of yourself being challenged. Don't fight it. Just say back to yourself – "I know – but it's fun pretending, isn't it?"

Exercise: MENTAL REHEARSAL No.1

Do use this whenever you need to prepare for an occasion when you want to shine – an interview, a meeting or a social occasion when you are meeting people for the first time. Perhaps you would like to demonstrate some quality that you doubt you possess, which doesn't feel quite *you*. Choose a person who represents that quality for you, someone who can be your role model. What role would you choose to play? This works better if it's more specific, e.g. Cary Grant because he's so smooth, Audrey Hepburn because she's so elegant, Colin Powell because he's so unflappable, Hillary Clinton[6] because she's so assertive.

However, it can work quite well if you just have a general idea – an executive, a leader, a movie star.

Play the whole scene out first in your imagination, as if you are that person. Since it's all in your mind, you don't need to worry if it's not quite right the first time. You can experiment, be inventive, take risks, with no fear of looking silly or exposing yourself to ridicule. Try things out. Ask yourself, what feels good for you? What makes you feel uncomfortable? If the latter, ask yourself why. Be honest with yourself. Is it because that behaviour is not right for you, or is it just because it's different and new for you?

When you are happy with the results, run through the whole scene several times mentally. You will find that, as a result of this mental preparation, you will be confident and at ease in the actual situation, as if you have already done it many times.[7]

CHAPTER 5

Hypnosis

"I'd like to believe it, BUT..."

Is this the nagging little voice that stops you opening up to new and exciting possibilities? This is your mental critic. No doubt you've discovered that the more you try to reason or argue against it, the stronger it becomes.

Probably the biggest block to creating new beliefs is this *critical* part of our mind – that part which is constantly running reality checks and putting on the brakes when it perceives something as *not true*.

Like everything else in our wondrous body-mind system, this critical factor has a positive survival function. It maintains the status quo, assessing new information by comparing it to this status quo, which it labels reality. It prevents flights of fantasy and preserves the social order. If it malfunctions, we develop psychoses. Schizophrenia, for example, occurs when the subject can no longer distinguish between his internal reality or fantasy world and the external one, agreed upon and accepted by society.

Unfortunately, this critical factor tends to take itself very seriously, and may continue to reject even desired, valuable new information, convinced it is necessary for our survival to do so. Thus an old belief pattern or paradigm, develops an armour-like rigidity, out of self defence. And there we are, stuck, in a belief that may have become detrimental to our health and well being.

Fortunately, there are ways around this block. It is possible to trick the critical mind into letting go control, or at least temporarily stepping aside, and not interfering with the creative process. One of the most powerful ways to do this is with hypnosis.

Let me reassure you immediately that the so-called power of hypnosis does not refer to the power of the hypnotist over his subject. The real power is already there; in the subject's own inner-conscious mind, an amazing source of wisdom, experience and creativity. Hypnosis is simply a highly efficient tool to help liberate this inner power. One almost universally accepted definition of hypnosis is "a state of mind in which the critical faculty of the human is bypassed and selective thinking established."[1]

Most people have an exaggerated opinion of the hypnotist's power from stage or television shows. It really does look like the subject on stage is obliged to follow the hypnotist's commands. This impression is deliberately encouraged because it makes for a good show. In fact, the participants, who have already volunteered to come up from the audience, have chosen to take part in the experience and continue to exercise their choice during the performance. By allowing their critical faculty to be suspended, they can more easily go along with the game; they can be less inhibited and more involved. However, if at any point they are asked to do something contrary to their sense of morality or survival, the critical faculty will again intervene.

"Always remember that the law of self-preservation is universal and it has never been repealed. It isn't repealed in Hypnosis."[2]

A good stage hypnotist will prepare the ground by ensuring that there is a good atmosphere and that the participants trust him, respect his authority, and *want* to follow his directions. He will arrange the hypnotic suggestions in order of difficulty, starting with those that are easiest to accept. Every time a subject finds it easy to go along with a suggestion, the hypnosis is deepened, and he is able to believe in suggestions further and further removed from reality. So at first, for example, he is asked to imagine differences in temperature, or mood changes. Although most subjects can readily accept this, some, still too mindful of their critical faculty, may yet refuse. To encourage them, the hypnotist, rather than saying, "You feel very hot..." or, "You can't stop laughing," will say, "*Act as if* you are feeling very hot," and, "*Pretend* you can't stop laughing." The critical faculty no longer feels obliged to object that it isn't true, and gracefully steps aside.

OF TWO MINDS

To understand why we seem to be playing off one part of the mind against the other, we need to understand how the outer (conscious) and inner (subconscious) parts of our mind function.

The inner, subconscious mind is a huge storehouse of experiences and emotions, the source of the energy that fuels our behaviour.

The outer, conscious mind is for understanding and putting in order the current world reality. It uses analysis and logic and must provide a rational reason for behaviour, even if it is not correct. Its role is to defend and maintain the status quo.

A clear example of this was provided in a short demonstration of hypnosis that I gave in front of a class. The subject did not want to leave the stage and return to his seat. His subconscious mind was responding to the post-hypnotic suggestion: "You are stuck to your seat and cannot get up." However, his conscious mind found that totally illogical, if not ridiculous, and had to invent a plausible reason why he was not moving. So he explained to me (and to the guffawing audience) that he really preferred to stay seated where he was, as he could much better see and hear everything that was happening, by being so close.

The same phenomenon can be demonstrated in split-brain experiments. In certain epileptic subjects, the treatment calls for the corpus callosum to be severed, thus separating the left and right brain hemispheres. Although the subject appears to continue functioning normally, there is no more communication between the hemispheres. This can be demonstrated in a spectacular fashion in carefully prepared experiments. When an instruction is given only to the right brain, the patient will carry out the required action. When asked why he did so, he will reply, "Because I felt like it," or, "The idea just came to me". The left-brain, where the speech centres are housed, is unaware of the instruction, but needs to explain the apparently irrational action, and invents a logical reason. Michael Gazzaniga, neuro-psychiatrist, calls this the "interpreter".[3]

I'm sure you will recognize this same mechanism, though much less dramatic, in our so-called normal functioning. We believe we are rational beings, but are usually acting out the dictates of our subconscious mind, trying to convince ourselves consciously that we are perfectly justified in doing so.

So, we could say that the critical factor of the mind has two functions – to stop suggestions entering the subconscious mind if they do not seem rational and to explain in a rational way behaviour that has arisen from the subconscious level.

If we recognise how this works in ourselves, we can use certain techniques such as make believe, role playing and metaphor (all common techniques in hypnotherapy). These allow us to intervene when what should be a useful defence mechanism becomes an unnecessary barrier.

PRETEND — A HYPNOTIC INDUCTION

One lesser-known method of inducing hypnosis, recorded in my original student manual, uses pretending as its basic element.[4]

In the Rehearsal Technique: "Subjects are told to 'play-act', pretend they are in hypnosis and to follow suggestions, acting like they were really in hypnosis... It is likely at some point, they will really start drifting into actual hypnosis." In my hand-written notes at the side, I have added, "Good for resistant clients."

I can testify myself, from the point of view of the subject, to the effectiveness of this technique. In one of my early training classes in the U.S. the whole group was supposed to work in pairs to test hypnotic depth, each taking in turn the role of hypnotist and subject. Our teacher, Dr. Richard Harte, told us, "It doesn't matter if you're not really deep in hypnosis, but since I want all six tests to be administered, just pretend, for the purposes of the exercise, that you are deep in hypnosis and are a very receptive subject." At the time I considered I was a rather resistant subject, since my critical faculty was over developed, but I was very good at pretending. I could do that! Sure enough, since the obligation to respond correctly had been removed, I slipped into one of the deepest and most responsive trances I had experienced so far. I was not even aware of when pretence became reality.

When the practice period was over, I not only felt delighted with my achievement, but also had become acutely aware of the power of the Just Pretend stratagem, even though it was presented as a simple ploy for getting through a practice session more efficiently.

I felt almost as if part of my inner mind was flashing lights and sounding gongs – "This is important!"

All my previous successful experiences of Make Believe clicked into connection. If a hypnotic trance, which normally requires subtle professional skills, can be induced by just pretending to be already in trance, what else is possible? How else can we use this same mechanism to short-circuit other resistances of the critical mind and produce other desired states of consciousness – such as joy, serenity, inspiration and enthusiasm?

I decided I was going to find out as much as possible about this innovative approach.

As a hypnosis instructor, I have now used this same technique many times in classroom situations, always to find that the students are surprised and delighted at how easily (and unexpectedly!) they entered deep trance levels.

I have recently seen this same approach put to use in a demonstration of stage hypnosis by Ormond McGill. Ormond is now 90 years old and is still performing![5] He is considered the dean of American hypnotists. He has eschewed the more sensational elements and developed a calm, impressive style of showmanship. Since he can no longer rush from one side of the stage to the other, to take care of his 20-odd volunteer subjects, he simply asked them all to fix their gaze on a lit candle, and then instructed them, "Pretend that you are falling into deep, deep hypnosis." Further suggestions followed, with atmospheric music, and before long, all eyes were shut. Then, "Pretend that your eyes are stuck together, tightly stuck together. That's right. Now pretend that you cannot open them – no matter how hard you try. You see? Isn't that amazing? Pretending transforms to believing, and believing transforms to reality."

Stage hypnotists have passed on their best trade secrets to practicing hypnotherapists. Dave Elman was a stage hypnotist who, in the 1950's and 1960's in the U.S., trained hundreds of doctors and dentists in his rapid techniques so they could use them readily in their own busy surgeries, with every possible type of patient. Since these professional people had no time to use the classic time-consuming techniques (fixation, monotony, rhythm, progressive relaxation, levitation) he taught them such techniques as his pretend stratagem.

"I'll show you a simple way to bypass your critical faculty, (and obtain eye-closure), without these methods. Close your eyes and pretend you can't open them. Keep on pretending, and while you are pretending, try to open your eyes. You'll find that it is impossible, if you are concentrating hard on the pretence. Now you know very well that you can open your eyes any time you change your mind and stop pretending. All the time that you were pretending that you could not open your eyes your sense of judgment (your critical faculty) was completely suspended concerning that particular action. You have obtained the same eye closure that you would if you had used the (longer) techniques... This can be done instantaneously." [6]

In one particular class, where some doctors had been complaining of their difficulties practicing autosuggestion, a doctor brought along his 3-year old daughter. He had taught her how to use autosuggestion to control the itching whenever she suffered from a nervous rash. I will quote the experience directly from Elman's book, as it provides a wonderful illustration of how easy and simple the pretend technique is. After all, if a child can do it...

"I asked the father of the child if he would let his daughter demonstrate before the group of doctors and he agreed. Then he said to his daughter, 'Honey, all these people here are doctors just like Daddy, and they want to learn to play the game you play when you have the rash. Would you be a good girl and stand up here in front of the room and show them how you do it, and as you do it, tell them how.' She said, 'All right, Daddy. First I have to have the itch and feel as if I want to scratch.' Her father said, 'All right, make believe you have the itch and want to scratch. Then what do you do?' She said, 'Well, now I make believe I have the itch and want to scratch, so I close my eyes like this.' She closed her eyes and continued, 'But I must make sure that I can't open them, so I play the game of make believe and now while I'm making believe that I can't open them, I try to open them, like this.' And she made a visible effort to open her eyes, without success. She went on, 'Now I know I can't open my eyes, so I say to myself, 'I won't itch any more and so I don't want to scratch.' Then I wait a little bit and I open my eyes when I stop playing the game, like this' – and she opened her eyes – 'and now I don't itch and I don't want to scratch.'" [7]

PRETEND AS THERAPY

Even if you have no intention of actually being hypnotised to achieve change, you can still use the hypnotist's trick of pretending so you can bypass the critical faculty when it is getting in your way! Although it is much easier in hypnosis, anyone can use make believe to experience more confidence, courage, motivation, energy and well being.

Some therapists may do this subtly through the use of metaphor; for example, telling a story about an eagle learning to fly. The client allows himself to experience vicariously courage, personal power, risk-taking – whatever he needs to take for himself.

Others use forms of Pretend Therapy which are much more overt. For example, in England, there is a course run over a seven-day retreat, conducted by a psychiatrist, a psychologist and a communications coach, for people who want to develop self-confidence. It's called the "Confidence Lab". One whole section of the course is called "Be Your Own Hero" and was filmed for BBC television.

Commentator: *Roy (the coach) finds that people often act with more confidence when they pretend to be someone else. He gives Jo (a participant) the chance to step into the shoes of someone she really admires.*

Roy: *Jo, who's your hero?*
Jo: *Dawn French.*
Roy: *What's heroic about Dawn French?*
Jo: *She draws people to her – she's full of confidence – she seems to be a character that people feel at ease with, and it's OK to be big!*
Roy: *All right then, what I'd like you to do is to imagine that you're your hero.*
Commentator: *In the session she took on the characteristics of her hero, Dawn French.*
(Later) **Roy:** *So, what's it like being Dawn?*
Jo: *It's quite good, actually, to have the permission to… to get out there and go.*
Roy: *To have permission from whom?*
Jo: *(Confused silence)*
Well, it was from you originally… but not to have to hold back.
Jo: *Let's assume that you have permission to be who you want to be – Who would you be?*

For the rest of the session, the others in the group encourage Jo to demonstrate the qualities that she admired in her hero, and wants to develop in herself. The results are remarkable, and Jo blossoms.

PARTS THERAPY

In a later chapter, we will see how Parts Therapy[8] can be used in hypnosis to allow the subject to act out several different roles, changing rapidly from one to the other. Each role is a part of his personality which may have been repressed, underdeveloped or unrecognised, or, on the other hand, which may have become too dominant and taken over.

By acting out each part, the subject is able to give full expression to a whole range of different possibilities that are within him, and to exercise a choice concerning which valuable parts of himself he wishes to develop. The results are quite dramatic – in every sense of the word! Since the critical faculty is bypassed, the subject in hypnotic trance has no trouble in acting as if each part is a separate personality in its own right. He will often produce a different voice, facial expressions and body posture for each one, as well as some new and creative ideas. The reaction afterwards is often, "Goodness, I didn't know that I had it in me!"

SELF-HYPNOSIS

To benefit from some of the ideas in this chapter, you do not necessarily have to go out and find a hypnotist. Everyone is capable of producing a light state of hypnosis by simply relaxing and focusing their attention. You do it already when driving for long periods, watching television, or becoming completely absorbed in a book.

By adding the element of make believe (and a three-year old child can do it!) and temporarily ignoring your critical faculty, you can experience totally new areas of yourself in your imagination.

Exercises

Exercise: BE YOUR OWN HERO!

Find yourself a time and place where you can be quiet with yourself. In a comfortable sitting position, eyes closed, think of the people you admire – your heroes. They could be world-famous or known only to you. Decide when and for how long you would like to be each person. For example: "Monday, I will be X, Tuesday, I will be Y, etc."

Do it, and enjoy yourself!

When, after a time, you have played several different heroes, sit down again and think about what qualities you most admire and which you most enjoyed acting out.

Give yourself permission to allow those qualities to become part of you. Continue practicing these qualities by pretending that you have them and you will find that the pretence becomes reality.

Exercise: PRETEND YOU CAN'T OPEN YOUR EYES

Use the hypnotist's trick to bypass your critical faculty. (Read again, if necessary, how the doctor's 3-year old daughter did this.)

First, in your quiet place, close your eyes. Relax your face, and especially your eye muscles. Relax them so much that you feel they won't work any more. Then pretend that you can't open them. Make believe the eyelids are stuck together. Test to make sure the eyes won't open.

When you have achieved this, give yourself positive suggestions – for good health, energy, self-confidence, concentration – whatever you feel you need but usually have difficulty believing and accepting.

Secondly, extend this to an active waking state. Select which hero or personality you would like to be. Decide for what period of time, or in what specific situation, you will make believe to be that person. As you start, say to yourself, "As long as I am pretending to be X, I remain confident and self-assured," or, "As long as I am pretending to be Y, I feel calm, relaxed and in control." It is important to use the present tense. This is the hypnotist's trick of bypassing the critical faculty and establishing selective thinking – focusing on the desired result.

You can, of course, stop pretending at any moment, but as long as you are pretending – it will work!

PART III
Multiple Selves

Introduction

If you could be anyone you liked, who would it be? Perhaps to become that person you can draw on characteristics you already have deep within. Who knows how many different people you are already?

In this section we look at how to discover these different selves. People who suffer from multiple personality syndrome can give us some clues. Psychodrama, Voice Dialogue and Parts Therapy all offer different approaches. Even the concept of past lives as hidden aspects of our own current personality can be useful. And finally, a résumé of different systems, recognised and respected for their effectiveness in switching on parts, will give you some practical ideas.

I would like you, throughout these chapters, to be aware of your *own* multiple selves – those parts of you that have become habitual and automatic, hence never questioned – those parts of you which have become overdeveloped and taken over – and those parts of you which you long to reveal, but never dared give expression.

Remember that you can change any and all of this, first by becoming aware that you *are* all these selves, and then by consciously choosing the parts you wish to play.

CHAPTER 6

Multiple Personality Syndrome

"You are a unique individual."

How many times have you heard that said to you? And, of course, you readily agree, because it is true – there is no one like you. But when you try to describe this individual, the definition probably becomes slippery. You may find yourself describing how sometimes you are highly extroverted and talkative, for example, but at other times you just like to be quietly on your own, to reflect. Or, most of the time you are serious and responsible, but sometimes you need to let down your hair and play around like a kid. It is impossible to define yourself as always being a certain type. You can only describe how you are likely to be at a given moment. This is because, no matter how stable and well balanced you may be, your individuality is actually a unique combination of many varied parts. *You* are, in fact, a multitude of different *yous*.

If you look back over your life for a moment, you will be aware of some of these different yous being dominant at different times. Obviously, you are different as a baby, a child, an adolescent and an adult. Other yous are associated with different stages – school, university, travel, different jobs, different relationships. Sometimes you will become a very different person according to your changing moods – momentary or long-lasting.

"Oh," you may laugh, when recalling a period when you were especially down, "that was my blue period."

That was *you*, but *not you*, because now *you* are different – again!

When moving from one area of your life to another – at home, at work, at leisure, at sport, with a hobby – you switch to the appropriate personality for your environment. We all do this to some extent, shifting gears almost automatically. Occasionally, some people will make a conscious decision to make a radical change, uprooting themselves from their past and starting again in a new country, or with a new religion, in an attempt to leave the old personality behind.

The extreme form of this phenomenon is known as Multiple Personality Disorder, also more recently referred to as Dissociative Identity Disorder.[1]

I wish to stress that this is recognised and classified as a mental illness, and is not to be confused with the wide range of behavioural differences included as normal, everyday functioning. These exist along a continuum until, at the extreme end we find the actual pathology – "disconnection from full awareness of self, time, and/or external circumstances."[2]

A brief look at this pathological condition should throw some light on our own, sometimes inexplicable everyday behaviour. After all, much of our modern understanding of mental health is based on Freud's observations of patients suffering from neurosis and hysteria.

It seems that a multiple personality is created when the original personality, as a child, is confronted with a situation that is too difficult to bear. Rather than risk dying in the face of unsupportable suffering, the identity splits[3] and creates a new personality capable of dealing with the situation – perhaps stronger, less emotional or more aggressive. This personality may take over temporarily or on a long-term basis, permitting the first personality to stay in hiding as long as it needs to protect itself. In the classic MPD cases, the patient has suffered a traumatic childhood, during which he may have created dozens of different personalities.

The human mind is amazingly creative in the construction of these defences – not only do the different personalities exhibit different emotions and behaviour, but they will claim to be a different age, sex or race!

In genuine MPD, each personality, or alter, has developed a completely independent personality from other alters, some of whom may be in conflict, while others are considered allies and/or helpers.

The syndrome first came to the general public's attention in the film "The Three Faces of Eve," based on a real life case study conducted by psychiatrist Corbett Thigpenn. [4]

Since then, such books as *Sybil* [5] (also made into a 1976 TV film) and *When Rabbit Howls* [6] have appeared, both written in association with therapists and based on real life case histories. These are both books that are easy to follow for the lay public and give an excellent idea of the causes, symptoms and treatment of MPD. Be warned, however, that the descriptions of child abuse and traumatic breakdown can be quite harrowing – not for the faint-hearted!

DR. HALL'S EXPERIMENT

I have already mentioned that Nicholas R.S. Hall, PhD, professor in the Department of Psychiatry and Behavioural Medicine at the University of South Florida, worked with a "multiple" to explore the effects of the mind on the body. [7]

The conclusions of this experiment suggest far-reaching possibilities for the general public. Is it possible to control our immune systems and other autonomic functioning?

Hall had wanted to demonstrate how a particular personality could impact the immune system and specific endocrine pathways. Unable to control all the variables present in a human, rather than an animal subject, he realised that a multiple personality was ideal to study this type of process. No matter how many distinct personalities exist, they all reside in the same body. "Consequently, all are exposed to the same level of exercise, to the same diet, and to the same over-the-counter medications." For the purposes of the study, a catheter was inserted into the subject's vein and multiple blood samples taken over a 4-hour period as the individual switched from one personality to another. The individual studied was a 32-year old woman with more than two dozen personalities, all different. "They ranged in age from 2 to 90; there was a Black, a Native American, male and female personalities, and even an animal personality. One of the personalities was referred to by the host as a 'healing personality'. When this individual was present, it didn't matter what disease existed at the time, the symptoms went away. Another personality, Cindy, was just the opposite. In fact, all of the other personalities tried to keep this personality out of the body because she was depressed, and the body always became ill whenever she was present."

Using such measures as lymphocyte blasto-genesis, Hall was able to observe marked differences in immune functioning between the individual personalities, sometimes in less than a minute – between the final sample of one personality and the initial sample of the next. These variations correlated with behavioural changes – facial expressions, body language and voice characteristics.

These studies were not continued, for several reasons, including a newly emergent personality who threatened to sue if the data was published!

OTHER OBSERVATIONS

Various other therapists report extraordinary findings with their MPD patients. Different personalities produce different brain-wave patterns, blood-flow and voice patterns. They will use different hands, changing from right to left, produce different handwriting and achieve different results in IQ tests. Some will smoke and others not; some need glasses and others not. Most remarkable are the apparent biological changes – medical conditions seem to come and go within a few seconds of personality change. There are documented cases of an allergic rash produced from orange juice, and swelling from a wasp sting, both mysteriously disappearing. Personalities exhibit different susceptibilities to drugs, alcohol and anaesthetics. Most mind-boggling are accounts of a diabetic, an epileptic and an HIV patient, all three diagnosed as having MPD, losing their illness when switched to another personality. [8]

Deidre Davis Brigham describes her astonishment when first witnessing this as a fledgling therapist.

"One morning 'Jill' came for her session with a terrible case of the flu. She could hardly breathe, her chest was congested, her nose was running, and she had laryngitis. She was a wheezing mess! During the session, I asked to talk to Jane, another of the personalities. In the six or so seconds it took for the transition, Jane appeared – with none of the symptoms Jill was manifesting! There was no congestion, she was able to speak normally, and there was no coughing or runny nose. When I asked her about this, she said, "Oh, I'm not the one who is sick, Jill is. She's so stupid, she's always catching something."[9]

In nearly all cases, multiples seem to heal faster than normal people.

All of them provide dramatic evidence that a change of perception can change the functioning and chemistry of one's body.

"This is all well and good," you may say, "even very impressive – but how does it help ME? After all, I'm just normal."

Indeed, all these examples are drawn from psycho-pathological cases – unfortunates who have been diagnosed with a mental illness. And you are normal, are you not?

However, most of the therapists working with MPD come to the same conclusion – that these extreme cases point to a potential that exists in every one of us.

We still do not understand HOW a multiple can control his/her body to the extent that he/she can just switch on and off complex autonomic processes. But we do know that "once a multiple has undergone therapy and in some way becomes whole again, he or she can still make these switches at will. **This suggests that somewhere in our psyches we *all* have the ability to control these things.**"[10]

Over the last 40 years, various therapies and self-development methods have been created which recognise and work with this potential in all of us.

Whereas the treatment of MPD attempts to integrate the personalities into a whole, these methods take into account that, in a normally functioning person, different parts exist, not just to hide from the world, but as a way of exploring life through different points of view.

These methods, some of which we will see in the next chapter, celebrate the wonderful flexibility and adaptability of the human spirit.

Exercises

Exercise: MULTIPLE YOUS

Sit down with a mug of hot coffee, the phone off the hook and a fresh, lined notebook. Look back over your life and divide it into large sections, according to changes in your lifestyle – health, education, profession, relationships. (For example, mark off a 3-year period when your job took you to another area.)

Then divide it into sub-sections, including this time personal interests and moods. (For example, within those three years you spent a period feeling lonely and depressed, then a wave of enthusiasm when you joined a new club, then a surge of new energy when you started jogging regularly.) You will be surprised to find how easily your life falls into natural divisions.

Looking over these, notice how certain aspects of your personality became dominant for awhile, then receded, then perhaps reappeared.

Which aspects are you proud of?

Which have you almost forgotten?

Which would you prefer to forget about, for shame or embarrassment? Which do you wish you could bring back?

It may amuse you to give names to these different aspects, or at least the time periods, to identify them more easily. Each aspect was an expression of *You*, at that time, and as such is still available, if you want it.

Close your eyes, take three deep slow breaths, and sink back in time to a period when you wish to reconnect with one particular aspect. Remember and relive the physical sensations, the thoughts and the emotions. Name the aspect (e.g. "This is the Passionate Me", or, "This is Joy"). Bring back these feelings with you to the present moment, and imagine yourself doing something in this time and place with the same qualities.

You can repeat this for many different aspects, which you will then be able to call up, using their names, when you need them.

CHAPTER 7

Discovering Your Parts

If you have ever argued with yourself, been beside yourself, or reacted out of character, you have exhibited some of the characteristics that define classic MPD.

The big difference is that you, being normal, don't believe that you actually have separate identities which take over and control you. Rather, you have certain tendencies, sub-personalities, or energy patterns, which will arise in certain circumstances. And you are *aware* that they exist! Sometimes you may not recognise it until after the event – "I don't know what came over me" – but you are quite conscious that it is still *you*.

It is conscious awareness that is the key to enabling us to take control of how our different parts interact. Once we can exercise *choice*, we are able to use the positive aspects of each part of us. We can decide which strength or sensibility or serenity, we wish to tap into, and pretend, consciously, that we become that part which has that quality.

Let us look at some of the different methods that have evolved.

PSYCHODRAMA

Developed in the 1940's by J.L. Moreno,[1] psychodrama and socio-drama are used in educational, health and business settings. Although various versions exist, in general this is carried out in a group setting, conducted by a trained practitioner known as the director. Individuals are given the chance to act out different roles and encouraged to get into the part, physically and vocally, as much as possible.

This is not to be confused with Drama Therapy, where putting on a play is used in a therapeutic context. Psychodrama is improvised role playing geared towards self-discovery and creativity, rather than developing acting skills.

"Group members take active parts in one another's dramas so that they bring it as close to life as possible. In this way they may generate and practice new behaviours and ways of thinking and test them out... without judgment. Thus long-frustrated desires or fears can be enacted and greater freedom experienced. Reversing into the role of another creates a fresh experience of the wider world. From time to time, each individual in a group can be a star. In experiencing and expressing themselves dramatically a greater sense of self-worth and ability to rise to life challenges are developed." [2]

In my own experience of psychodrama, organised for a group of educational counsellors, the approach was much more like Gestalt chair therapy, where the emphasis is more on acting out inner, subjective experience.

In this case, the roles played were of those people who had exercised some influence over our lives – a parent, a teacher or a spouse, for example. If that influence still had a negative hold over us, we were given a chance to have it out in public. By switching backwards and forwards from the role of the old influence, with other group members playing the opposing figure, one could play out extraordinary scenes of unresolved tension – accusations, recriminations, tears, justifications, apologies, demands, denials – all flew back and forth in an exchange which, although make believe, allowed one to identify very real problems.

Whether one played the role of the opponent in an accurate manner had no importance at all for the therapeutic process. After all, this was not an acting class. The role being played was not actually another person, but our perception of that person, which could be quite different from objective reality. We invested the role with life and energy because we were in fact projecting onto that person all our own fantasies, desires and frustrations. Sometimes it is so much easier to blame an outside cause than admit the problem is in ourself! Even when the outside influence has long departed from our lives, we are left with a sort of psychic knot where that person is concerned.

This is where psychodrama really comes into its own. Old agendas can be completed, including grieving, trauma and resentment. Depending on the therapist/director, the participant can be encouraged to let it all out – telling the other all the things he or she has never been able to say in real life, unbottling all the pent-up emotions, sometimes even screaming, yelling, hitting out.

Then, change roles! Now one takes the role of the accused. What follows may be an explanation of what happened – "I thought I was acting for your own good"; a defence – "But I had no idea, I didn't understand"; a request for forgiveness – "I'm so sorry, please forgive me"; or an outright rejection – "You silly bitch! You had it coming to you."

In most cases, a reconciliation is achieved, however, this last aggressive reaction was more or less what I found myself declaring when role-playing an ex-partner who had been extremely domineering and controlling (when I was much younger!) By connecting with, and expressing, what I considered to be his energy, I was able to externalise those elements of him that I had taken into myself.

So even though, in this case, no reconciliation was possible, it still led to a new awareness and a new freedom. Although the whole process is make believe it leads to a very real step in freeing yourself from the past and reclaiming your own power.

SOCIODRAMA

This form of psychodrama is used for developing social awareness and resolving social issues. Rather than focusing on the drama of a single protagonist, this process allows the group as a whole to explore various situations in a safe, structured environment. For example, a group of managers at a conference might wish to explore a future strategic plan; a group of unemployed people might want to learn how to act during a job interview; a group of school social workers might enact a scene where a family confronts staff concerning their child's behaviour. "The concept underlying this approach is the recognition that man is a role player, that every individual is characterised by a certain range of roles which dominates his behaviour and that every culture is characterised by a certain set of roles which it imposes with a varying degree of success upon its members." J.L. Moreno [3]

During my years working with the Southern Australian Department of Education I had the great pleasure and good fortune to be part of the Theatre-in-Education team. Our mandate was to create short plays for different age groups and to perform them within actual school classrooms for the purpose of developing social awareness. At one stage, for example, we developed a piece on sexual harassment, when it was considered a political and social hot potato. Although not socio-drama to the extent that adolescents in the audience were themselves part of the performance, they were able to intervene at different points and affect the actual outcome. A scene would be stopped and put on hold while the spectators addressed the characters directly and gave their opinions. Then the scene would be continued, or repeated in a different way, according to the spectators' suggestions. At this point, of course, we as actors had to improvise whatever was thrown at us. It made for some very exciting inter-active theatre, as well as providing a chance for the teenagers watching to identify with the protagonists and to test other ways of behaving. While they remained in the safety of their seats, they could watch the actors play out possible solutions. We could sense how empowering it was for them to realise that no one need be a victim of circumstances – that other alternatives are always available!

VOICE DIALOGUE

This was developed in the 1980's by Hal Stone and Sidra Winkelman, and described in their excellent book, *Embracing Our Selves*.

"The course of our lives is determined, to a considerable extent, by an array of selves that lives within each of us. These selves call out to us constantly – in our dreams and fantasies, in our moods and maladies and in a multitude of unpredictable and inexplicable reactions to the world around us. The more sharply we become attuned to these inner voices, the more *real* choice we are able to exercise in the pursuit of our individual destinies."[4]

Voice Dialogue is based on the idea that we each have archetypal energies within us, which can be identified with the Greek Gods – the rationality of Apollo, the libertine instincts of Dionysus, the power of Zeus, the maternal qualities of Hera, the belligerence of Ares/Mars, the sexuality of Aphrodite/Venus. This is called a Voice, as each energy is a way of *expressing* ourselves. The Stones identified certain Voices which are common to most of us – the Protector/Controller, the

Pleaser, the Parent, the Critic, the Inner Child, the Pusher – and suggest ways we can recognise, acknowledge and respect each Voice to reduce conflict and wasted energy.

Generally, a facilitator will first have a discussion with the client about the nature of the problem or area to be worked on. During this time, he will observe closely for any sign of conflicting emotions. He will then say, for example, "There seems to be a part of you that is annoyed that you have so many obligations to meet. I would like to hear what that part has to say." He then invites the client to move around the room, trying different stances or positions, until he feels that he is in character, as it were, and is able to literally give voice to those particular feelings. Eventually various room areas are designated for each Voice, which can be triggered by walking round to different positions or chairs.

My first experience of this, in a group workshop, was quite an eye-opener. My acting background made it easy – I took to it like a duck to water! But even though I was fully conscious of what I was doing, I was surprised at how spontaneously a Voice would express itself, changing physical attitude and vocal quality as appropriate. At one point I found myself yelling at myself – in frustration – "Suffer, baby!" But *who* was yelling at *whom*?

The facilitator pointed out that it was important to listen to each Voice as it expressed itself. When a Voice was ignored it could cause psychic damage. When recognised and respected, (though not necessarily given its way!) it could contribute to the well-being and success of the whole person. The part of us that remains an objective observer and helps each Voice to cooperate with the others is known as the Aware Ego. The more the Ego is Aware, the less it identifies with any particular part.

Once the client is sensitised to recognise the shifts in energy patterns that indicate the expression of a new sub-personality, he or she can carry out inner dialogues. He/she can, for example, ask one Voice what it suggests as a solution when another Voice is stuck. At no time is there a notion of separate entity – rather the recognition of different processes at work within the many-layered mind. Allotting names and roles to each Voice is all part of a conscious pretence which allows one to fully experience the different available energies.

PARTS THERAPY

One of the most powerful of these techniques, especially as it is conducted in a deep hypnotic state, is Parts Therapy, also known as Parts Integration Therapy, or Ego States Therapy. This was developed in the 1960's by Charles Tebbetts [5] and is now promulgated by his protégé, Roy Hunter [6].

This system recognises that each and every one of us has different parts, or sub-personalities, of which we are quite conscious, but which we are not always able to control e.g. "I really need to go on a holiday, but part of me won't let me," or, "Part of me wants to lose weight, but another part won't stop eating."

Parts Therapy may be called for, and prove highly efficient, when there is an unresolved inner conflict, or when the client is self-sabotaging. The hypnotist then uses deep trance state to allow the client to recognise that those parts exist, and then acts as a mediator, guiding the different parts in a discussion until resolution is achieved.

"Competent Parts Therapy is similar to facilitating mediation between conflicting people, except that the conflict is between *parts of the subconscious* rather than between different people with disagreements. Just as in actual mediation, the therapist must *remain objective*, allowing all appropriate parts of the inner mind to both speak and listen to any or all other parts wishing to express and be heard." [7]

During a typical session of Parts Therapy the hypnotist will first make sure that the client understands that it is completely normal for all of us to have different parts, and that hypnosis can help him by calling some of these parts out into conscious awareness. The fact that this happens is *not* an indication of Multiple Personality Disorder!

Once the subject is in trance, the hypnotist indicates that he would like to speak to one of the parts in conflict. This could be either the part that wants change, or the part that is resisting (e.g. the smoker or the non-smoker).

The hypnotist is careful to gain rapport with each part right from the start. He recognises that the part has an important role to play and is doing what it considers best for the total good of the client. He treats it as an individual worthy of respect, thanks it for coming, and asks its name and purpose. At no stage does the hypnotist judge or criticise. This could lead to a part's refusal to cooperate, and an even worse impasse than before!

Once each part has had its say, it is now the hypnotist's job to act as mediator. This can require highly complex negotiating and conflict resolution skills, just as in any group situation. (At least one advantage is that not everyone will talk at once, as there is only one mouth available!) Arguments may rage back and forth, and sometimes other parts may need to be called in to add their opinion. The hypnotist, with gentle leading and questioning, brings them to a mutual understanding and an agreement, even if this must be a compromise. No part must be made to feel it is ignored or neglected.

A case study quoted by Charles Tebbetts gives a clear example. In one session he was able to cure a businessman who had suffered for many years from chronic migraines.

"I called out the part that was causing the trouble, which called itself the power plant. It told me it was going to keep right on with its behaviour, both to punish and protect Joe. I then asked the part that wanted to be free of the headaches to talk to the power plant and explain how it felt. Rather than addressing Joe, power plant explained to me: 'Joe is like a little machine, thinking and planning, how to make more money. How to get ahead. He even plans and thinks in his sleep. I give him nightmares and awaken him with a headache so he can't work the next day, and I'm going to keep it up until he slows down.'

I told Joe, 'You heard what the power plant said. Maybe if you slow down he might quit punishing you.'

Joe's answer was, 'But I've tried to slow down. My main interest in life is planning moneymaking deals and investments. That is my hobby.'

My answer was, 'Do you do much thinking and planning while you are having the headaches?'"

Both parts continued to justify their actions until the hypnotist helped them to make a deal. It was suggested that Joe "choose a certain number of hours a day for planning and thinking about getting ahead, and enjoy those hours to the fullest. Then relax and enjoy the rest of the time, the time (he) used to suffer with the headaches... Joe agreed to follow these suggestions, and the power plant agreed to quit punishing him as long as he kept his agreement. Joe moved to the East Coast, and gave me a number of phone calls to tell me that one session had been a complete success." [8]

Sometimes, two parts will be at complete loggerheads and refuse to budge from their position. In this case, an appeal may be made for another part to come out, which is in closer connection with Higher Consciousness, or Inner Wisdom, or whatever corresponds to the client's own belief system. In this way, the solution always comes from the client's own inner consciousness, not from the advice or recommendation of the hypnotist. [9]

Once an agreement has been reached, the part that used to be concerned with punishing or interfering may choose to take on a new name and a new job, if appropriate. Thus the energy is re-channeled in a positive direction. In conclusion, the different parts are encouraged to work in harmony for the well-being of the whole person.

Whether for epileptic fits or for simple time-management, Parts Therapy has proved itself a powerful technique for conflict resolution.

How can this complex and challenging therapy be of benefit to you? Without needing to make an appointment with a hypnotist, the concept alone – that you are many different parts – is extremely healthy and beneficial. You must realise that you are not condemned to be stuck in any situation or behaviour because of your so-called personality. You have, in fact, many personalities. You can choose, consciously, which one you need at the current moment to influence or guide you. Some ideas of how to do this are presented in the practical exercises that follow.

Exercises

Exercise: TOTEM ANIMALS

(Thanks to Jerry Seavey for this exercise) [10]

In a quiet, meditative state, go through each of your chakras, starting with the base of the spine, then the stomach, the solar plexus, the heart area, the throat, the forehead, and the crown of the head. Concentrating on each area in turn, "call forth" an animal, allowing the first animal that springs to mind to be that particular totem. You will probably find that you have widely differing animals, including birds, reptiles, even fish!

Then imagine you call them together for a meeting. In a natural clearing, visualise each of the animals arriving and choosing a position in a circle that seems appropriate, with respect to where you stand. You will be eight in the circle. Allow the animals to change around if they wish. Perhaps there are some disagreements – allow the animals to defend their positions and to put their point of view to the rest of the group.

Continue till each animal has found its place to its own satisfaction and with the agreement of all members. You will have made some interesting discoveries about yourself and your archetypal energies, and will have achieved a state of harmony and balance.

Exercise: MEET YOURSELVES, OR, CONFLICT RESOLUTION

(Although this is much easier with an outside facilitator, with an active, trained imagination, you can work well on your own.)

Again, in a quiet, meditative state, specify the nature of your problem, e.g. "I would like to make a success of my business, but part of me keeps intervening and tripping me up." Or, "I would like to stop smoking, and know it's important for my health, but part of me can't resist cigarettes and refuses to stop!"

Designate clearly the part that seems to be creating the conflict, and recognise that it has its own reasons, and, in its own way, must be working for your good. Say you would like to talk to it, and hear what it has to say.

Imagine an inner voice, representing this particular energy, expressing itself as it really wants to. Ask its name and its role. Enter into a dialogue, explaining what your needs are, but equally listening to its point of view.

Perhaps other parts will pop up, with other points of view. Allow each to have its say, and bring all the parts into some sort of working agreement.

Even if there is lack of trust and respect amongst some of the different parts, they may well accept a compromise for the good of the whole. The situation can then be reviewed in a week or a month's time.

Remember to enjoy yourself and give free rein to your imagination. Surprise yourself!

CHAPTER 8

Past Lives

"Who do you want to be?"

This is a question I've asked you several times throughout this book. Now, just for a moment, let's ask, "Who *did* you want to be?" That is, if you *could have been* someone else in a past life, whom would you choose? In this life you have certain restrictions imposed by your birth into this current body, country, period in time. But, if you had the whole of history to choose from, and you could be someone more exotic, wealthy, wise or famous than you are now, who would it be?

Before we go any further, please don't reject this chapter out of hand because you "don't believe in reincarnation." Whether you believe in it or not makes no difference whatsoever. I would just like you to entertain the idea of having been other people as a useful tool for becoming more yourself today, for literally expanding your consciousness to overcome self-imposed limitations.

I have known people so caught up in their belief in a previous life – "I was the seventh daughter of Akhenaten!" – that they spend all their time and energy in this current life defending their position, even arguing heatedly with others who claim the same incarnation! Like all extremes, this is decidedly unhealthy and becomes an escape from reality.

My own point of view is that, since we can never really know, it is more useful and beneficial to simply play with the idea – "I wonder if..." – so long as it helps us to lead a richer and fuller life in the here and now.

When I was much younger and had an unusual medley of different friends and acquaintances, I was invited to a "come-as-you-were party". You have heard, no doubt, of a "come-as-you-*are*-party", when the guests arrive spontaneously, dressed in whatever outfit they are wearing when called – be it pyjamas, gardening shorts, whatever. The cleverly named "come-as-you-were party" was actually a fancy dress party with a theme – guests were asked to arrive in costume, and in character, representing a previous life. An amazing motley of characters turned up – ancient Egyptians, Greeks and Romans in sheeted togas, witches and wizards, royalty and shepherds, Indians, Spaniards and Asians. As you can imagine, it was quite an ice-breaker. Total strangers were immediately chatting animatedly, asking questions and swapping anecdotes. Some of the guests who thought it was just a fun idea were quite bemused by others who seemed to take the whole thing quite seriously.

Your reaction to this could well be, "How pathetic! They all want to be someone else. They can't accept the reality of their own petty little lives."

But look a little further. Somewhere in there is the recognition, even if distorted in some cases, that they have the possibility to be MORE.

Look at the young woman playing Egyptian princess, for example. What does she get out of it? She knows she's not REALLY a princess – she's just May Stubbs, part-time waitress, full-time wife and mother. But dressed up and playing this role, there is a sparkle of new life in her eyes. She moves with a dignity and an assurance that she would never ALLOW ordinary little May Stubbs. It is nevertheless, *her* dignity – habitually hidden, repressed, considered, "Oh no, that's not me!" Now she can give full reign to this specific quality that she needs in her life. No one else could make believe that particular dignity which is special and unique to her, and to which she can only give expression when she is pretending to be someone else.

Look at that middle-aged man wearing a helmet and sword and false beard, all done up as an ancient warrior. In real life he is a clerk, rather colourless and unassuming. Here, somehow, he seems to have grown much bigger. His shoulders are thrown back, his head held high. He is laughing with a deep-throated booming voice that surprises those who know his normal meek, quiet tones. What a wonderful chance to express all the energy, courage and virility that are normally suppressed, considered inappropriate for his professional role.

And look over there – goodness, that can't be Lucy, the grocer's assistant! She is almost unrecognisable out of her habitual grey smock, hair pulled tightly back. Now she is flaunting her body in glorious techni-colour, and her luxurious hair is cascading wildly round her face and shoulders. She is a gypsy fortune-teller, complete with huge gold ear-rings, tassels and crystal ball, and she is playing it to the hilt. She is having the time of her life!

If Shirley MacLaine[1] were here, it would be her sort of party! I won-der who, a hundred years from now, will remember having been Shirley MacLaine in a previous life!

We each of us have, within us, the potential of all humanity, but we restrict ourselves to playing such a limited number of roles, usually pre-determined. Foolish imaginings they may well be, our daydreams of other lives, but surely no more foolish than accepting the concept of one little box of a life which others have imposed upon us.

What we call fantasy is a double-edged sword – depending on whether we use it to cut ourselves off from reality, or to cut open reali-ty to release the deeper riches and magic hidden within.

In the U.S. in the late 1980's, inspired by Dr. Brian Weiss's book, *Many Lives, Many Masters*,[2] a new rage for Past Life Therapy developed. It is estimated that there are today in the U.S. at least 2,000 Past Life Therapists – and about half of them do not believe in reincarnation! Are they, then, hypocrites, taking advantage of a popular fad to line their own pockets? Not at all. They are serious, dedicated professionals who are prepared to use the technique because it works! Certain patients, who can be stuck for years with a problem, can be completely cured in one session of past-life hypnotic regression, where they are told to go back in time to the source of their problem. Having identi-fied the cause, and having understood that it comes from a previous lifetime, which no longer exists, the patient is liberated from the prob-lem, whether it be anxiety, phobia, guilt, obsession or psychosomatic symptom, and feels capable of leading a new life. If he/she knows, for example, that a fear of water comes from drowning in a previous life, then he/she knows that he/she no longer needs this fear in the present.

Whether the experience is real or fantasy has no importance. What counts is the result – the patient is cured. As one psychotherapist explained, the mind has a self-healing capacity and is able to create metaphors that, especially when vividly experienced, lead to physical and emotional correction.

Just one example from my own case files:

One of my students was suffering from allergic reactions from nearly everything she ate, and it was getting worse! She asked for a regression to the cause, and, although I was expecting a childhood experience, snapped back spontaneously to a previous lifetime where, bound hand and foot in a medieval forest setting, she was being forced to drink a poisonous scalding mixture from a boiling cauldron. Once she had re-lived the burning sensation in her throat and the subsequent body reactions before dying, she realised that this had carried through as a fear that anything she ate would poison her! One hour later, she was happily tucking into a restaurant lunch with the rest of the students – with no allergic reaction!

In my own classes, I also encourage those students who wish to use Past Life Therapy to experiment with some more positive aspects. Regressing to the cause of a problem usually reveals a painful, even traumatic event. However, they can also regress a client to a more pleasant past life, where he or she had developed a creative gift or an artistic capacity, to reconnect with it and bring it back to the current life. Thus latent talents can be explored and developed, with the added confidence that, "Well, I've done that already and I was brilliant at it!" Some amazingly creative ideas and inspiration can also be tapped with this method, and new sources of energy accessed and released.

If you find this idea pleasing or intriguing, please turn to the exercise PAST LIFE TALENT at the end of this chapter. What I do not encourage is Past Life "Tourism", when the subject is motivated simply by curiosity – "I wonder who I could have been?" This sort of speculation risks developing into a pure ego-trip.

Another idea explored by far fewer therapists is that of Progression into a future life.[3] This is loosely based on the quantum physics concept that time, which is perceived as linear, actually all exists in the present moment. So, in theory, we can remember the future! Already it is reassuring to believe that we can make up for this life's disappointments and failings in a later life, where circumstances will be different. Even better, then, to undergo this future life as a vivid personal experience, especially if it brings hope and encouragement to the present.

Things will definitely get better!

In fact, this technique of visualising oneself in a better future, in this lifetime, is a standard technique in many personal development programmes. It can be a few days away, or many years, but identification with this future self provides the motivating fuel to set and achieve valuable goals. Some specific examples will follow in chapter 11, THE MAGIC WORD "IF".

Since a past (or future) life can never be proven, let us not concern ourselves too much with the reality of the experience. It is the psychological reality and the positive results, which are important. If pretending to be someone else temporarily is beneficial, then the possibility of reincarnation opens the doors to the whole of human history – a multitude of different selves which we can continue to access, for ever richer and deeper resources for living.

Exercises

Exercise: PAST LIFE TALENT

This exercise can be used repeatedly. Allow yourself at least 15 minutes every time you do it.

Decide first what is the purpose of your search. What is the creative talent you want to connect with? It could be a hobby, a sport, writing, painting, healing and helping others.

With eyes closed, allow yourself to relax into a daydreaming state.

Tell yourself you want to go back to a previous lifetime when you had this particular talent. Allow your mind to wander freely, and follow your first impressions. Continue daydreaming.

If the first idea that comes to mind is a famous figure, don't block it by protesting, "That couldn't possibly be me!" After all, for the purposes of this exercise, you are just pretending! Some images may seem silly, others productive. Don't judge, but go with the flow.

When you drift back to wakefulness, write down in a notebook the main ideas and impressions that have come to you. When you look back at these notes a day or so later, you may be surprised at how profound they are.

Exercise: YOUR SOUL'S DESIRE

To discover (or remember) your mission, the real reason why you came into this lifetime. This exercise is distilled from a one-day workshop.

First, do a little preparation – even over several days – by asking yourself who are the figures in history or the present that really inspire you. Would you like to be that person? What are their personal qualities that resonate with you? What have they done to make a difference on the planet? It can also be just as revelatory to ask yourself the opposite – who are the figures that represent the other pole, those who you would NEVER want to be?

Now, choose a quiet time and place when you will not be interrupted, to make a long journey in your imagination. Make believe for a moment that reincarnation is real, and that you chose to incarnate at this particular time and place as this particular person. Why did you choose to be you? What is the potential to be filled in this particular lifetime you have chosen? Are you filling it? Or have you forgotten? It may help to record your own voice onto a cassette tape, so that you can guide yourself, give instructions and ask appropriate questions.

With your eyes closed, take several deep breaths. Allow your body to relax, from the head all the way down to the toes. Feel your body sinking softly down into the armchair where you are sitting or the bed on which you are lying. Allow your mind to drift back in time, recalling happy moments from last year, first job, high school, primary school, your first childhood memory.

Then feel yourself drawn way back, as if through a tunnel and into a beautiful white light, the spiritual region between lives. Here your consciousness includes the memory of all your past lives, and the knowledge of what you want and need to do in your next incarnation. You are preparing to be born into your current body. Your purpose is clear to you.

Imagine you are now choosing the life to come, a life which will allow you to accomplish your mission, while learning the appropriate lessons for your soul's development. It is as if you can see the whole planet Earth floating in space.

 … You now choose which country, and which culture you will be born into.
 … You choose which sex and what sort of body you will have.
 … You choose your mother, and your father.
 … You choose the people whom you will meet that will influence your life – friends, teachers, mentors.
 … You choose the situations and events that will mark you.
 … You choose your education, your profession.

At each stage, ask yourself why you are choosing this – how can this help you to evolve and to achieve your mission? You see a pattern emerging and a clear direction in your life, in spite of all the petty details and upsets which will distract you when you are immersed in daily life.

As you emerge from this experience, give yourself time to reflect and to make notes of your impressions. You may achieve very deep and powerful understandings as a result of this exercise.

CHAPTER 9

Infinite Variety

How many *selves* are we, really?

It seems the possibilities are infinite – just as there are infinite different methods for recognising and developing those selves. So far, I have mentioned Multiple Personalities, Parts Therapies and Past Lives.

Here, I will touch on just a few more, with the qualification that my selection is based on the chance encounters of my own personal experience. I am sure that you, also, will be able to think of many other areas where this concept is found.

FREUD

Freud based his whole system of psychoanalysis on the concept of Id, Ego and Super-Ego, three parts of our psyche that can be in conflict with each other, and must be recognised and balanced. The Id harbours primitive instincts of the body, like sex and aggression, and functions entirely according to the pleasure-pain principle at an unconscious level. The Ego is that portion which is experienced as the *self* or *I* and is in contact with the external world through perception. It remembers, evaluates, plans and reacts. The Super-Ego, the latest developing of the three agencies, contains a system of prohibitions, condemnations and inhibitions, known as the *conscience* as well as a set of ideals, inherited from parent-figures and society.

TRANSACTIONAL ANALYSIS

The American psychiatrist Eric Berne (1910-1970), founder of Transactional Analysis, posited that each of us contains three basic ego-states, which he called the Adult, the Parent and the Child. The Adult is mature, balanced, using logic, reason and conscious choice. It is able to objectively examine both the environment (external reality) and the thought processes (internal reality). The Parent is protective, criticising and judgmental. It is based on what we have observed in grown-ups and inherited from them. The Child is spontaneous, selfish and uncontrollable. This is the little boy or girl who takes over when we are scared – or when we just want to have fun! The goal of the approach is to develop a strong sense of maturity by learning to recognise the child and parent aspects of personality in yourself and others.

NLP RE-FRAMING

The classic six-step reframe of Neuro-Linguistic Programming described in *Frogs into Princes* [1] is very similar to the Parts Therapy described in the chapter before last. Although no formal trance state is used, the facilitator, after identifying the pattern of behaviour to be changed, asks to communicate with the part which is responsible for the pattern. He then determines what the positive intention is behind the problem behaviour, and negotiates with that part and the creative part to find other ways of achieving the same result, the positive goal desired. When the part is willing to take responsibility for generating alternative behaviour, he checks to make sure that there is no other part that objects.

SIX HATS

Edward de Bono, leading international authority on thinking skills and originator of the concept of Lateral Thinking, proposes a novel idea to stimulate creativity. Inspired by the expression, "Let me put on my thinking hat," he describes six different hats, each with its own colour, to denote different aspects of the personality.

"The first value of the six thinking hats is that of defined *role playing*. The main restriction on thinking is ego-defence, which is responsible for most of the practical faults of thinking. The hats allow us to think and say things that we could not otherwise think and say without risking our egos. Wearing the clown costume gives you full permission to play the clown." [2]

The White Hat is neutral and objective. It is concerned with objective facts and figures, like a computer, without any interpretations or opinions.

The Red Hat gives the emotional view, expressing personal opinions. It has strong feelings for or against an idea, and is also capable of subtle hunches and intuition.

The Yellow Hat is sunny, positive and optimistic about the outcome. It is constructive and generative, allowing both logical thinking and dreaming.

The Black Hat is negative. It covers all the reasons why it cannot be done. It plays the devil's advocate, pointing out errors and difficulties.

The Green Hat is connected with natural abundance and fertile growth. It indicates creativity and new ideas – going beyond the known and the obvious, searching for alternatives.

The Blue Hat is cool and takes an overview, concerned with controlling and organising the thinking process, including the other hats. It defines the subject, sets the focus and calls for conclusions. It is like the conductor of the orchestra.

To stimulate creativity, solve problems, facilitate brainstorming sessions, break down attitudinal barriers, de Bono suggests we deliberately choose to change hats. When the problem is perceived from a totally different viewpoint and we have been able to note down the insights obtained, we then switch hats and go on switching until we have a wealth of new ideas and resources to tackle the task.

YOUR COUNSELLORS

For many years I have taught the Silva Method, a self-help and mental development class based on getting into a relaxed, lightly altered state, getting to know yourself and knowing how to talk to your inner self. One of the most powerful exercises is called "Creating your Counsellors". I have since come across other versions, but still find this one of the best examples in its imaginativeness and clarity of intention.

By the third day of the class, you have already constructed an imaginary place, a workshop/laboratory with tools and equipment that represent symbolically your own mental faculties. You then invite first a male, and then a female counsellor to come and stay, via a lift-like compartment whose door descends gradually to reveal, bit by bit, the counsellor's appearance. This gives plenty of time to imagine what the counsellor could look like. Since they represent your own genius potential or Inner Wisdom, you may choose from any real or fictitious personality, modern or historic, who represents the qualities you admire in a genius. It could be Leonardo da Vinci, Gandhi or your Aunt Maud.

They play the same role as Saints, Ancestors, Spirit Guides, Guardian Angels – or Jiminy Cricket! They represent *You* (animus/anima, Yin/Yang, Creative/Receptive) with all your untapped resources and strengths – now available. To access this potential, you simply imagine you are talking to them, asking questions, discussing problems, seeking advice. Where normally your lack of confidence in your own self blocks you – "I couldn't possibly know/be/do that!" – your counsellor is everything you would be if you were wiser, stronger, braver, more talented and more experienced. When you imagine how they might reply to you, all sorts of ideas just pop into your head. It is a simple, fun and effective way to access deep levels of your inner self. It is, quite literally, a conscious-expanding exercise.

No doubt you have heard of many examples of channeling, where the speaker will go into a trance-like state and channel words of wisdom or advice from another entity, usually identified as a Spirit Guide or as an Extra-Terrestrial. I prefer not to enter into a discussion of the reality of these teachings. In my personal opinion, much of what is being channelled is coming from the speaker's own inner wisdom. This can be more easily accessed when the belief system is freed up by attributing the information to someone else, who has more authority than the individual dares attribute to him/herself.

OTHER DIMENSIONS

Research in quantum physics has given rise to the hypothesis of other dimensions that exist alongside ours, in a different time-space continuum. In these other dimensions exist all the other possibilities that could have taken place at any given moment, split off and developed in a different direction.

Thus in one other dimension you could be a king, in another a lawyer, or a doctor, an artist, a labourer, a pauper – the possibilities are, literally, infinite. If you could imagine that somewhere, in one of these dimensions, there exists a *You* who has *already developed* the knowledge and the skills that you are seeking now – then you could also imagine making a connection with that other you, in that other dimension. You could imagine picking their brains, sharing their experience, stepping into their body, to integrate this precious information into your own being. After all, it is you yourself; you would happily help yourself out, would you not?

At the time of writing, two well-known physicists, Jean-Pierre Garnier Malet and Philippe Bobola are presenting a new self-development course in Europe, based on their scientific publication, "The Doubling Theory".[3] It includes this idea of multiple dimensions, where each of us can access our "double".

Meanwhile, on the other side of the Atlantic, my friend and colleague Burt Goldman is presenting his new seminar, "Parallel Dimension Quest" where he too, asks his participants to use the concept of a "Doppelganger" or double.

Ah, synchronicity!

CONCLUSION

To conclude, the concept of Multiple Selves covers a gamut of experiences stretching from crippling mental illness to sophisticated systems of mental and spiritual development. The danger lies in allowing the self to *identify* with any one role or personality, and falling asleep in that identity. Like fire or electricity, our human role-playing tendency can be a bad master or a useful servant.

When you consciously use the concept, always developing more self-mastery and knowledge, it can open doors toward extraordinary personal and spiritual evolution. But, if you become too involved, you cannot become evolved. The key is conscious awareness. That way, anything that is in the human condition is available to you as a learning experience. Just don't become it! As the Sufis say, "When you *are* angry, you *become* anger; when you *experience* anger, you choose and you learn."

Be aware, remember consciously that you are just pretending or playing a role, and you will continue to learn and to grow. As if you are watching a movie – don't identify so much with the characters that you lose yourself – just remain aware and enjoy the movie!

If we are a living expression of the Divine, or the Life Force, then we are like the millions of different shining droplets in a giant fountain. We can choose to identify with just one droplet, or with a multitude. The choices are infinite.

Exercises

Exercise: AWARENESS

This is based on an old Sufi discipline.

Pick a specific routine activity that you do at fairly regular intervals during the day, (e.g. going through a doorway, putting on or taking off a coat), and practice awareness for the next 3 minutes.

Pay attention to everything you are doing – your gestures, your position, your words, your voice, even your thoughts. Don't criticise or comment, just observe.

Be fully conscious of the here and now, and what you are choosing to do in it. "I am now standing up, I am now turning around, I am now taking one step after another, I am now lifting my hand toward the door..."

Don't even attempt more than 3 minutes at first, as your untrained mind will find that even for this short time, it is already difficult not to wander off and be distracted.

If this happens, gently bring it back. "I am now taking a deep breath."

You may be surprised to find how much your mind is usually cluttered with trivia, and how little you are aware of what you are actually doing. As you train yourself to be more aware, observe when you unconsciously slip into certain energy patterns.

Someone criticises you, for example, and you find yourself replying in a drifting high-pitched voice, like that of a little girl. Or, perhaps the opposite: you find yourself bristling with rage, your muscles rigid, your chest tight, your hands clenched, in warrior mode, ready to defend yourself.

It can be quite alarming to discover how much of our lives we just follow stimulus-response patterns, acting (or reacting) like automatons. Once you start developing conscious awareness, you start to take charge of your life. You are no longer at the mercy of your habit patterns.

Exercise: WHICH HAT?

Try this when you are stumped, or stuck in a particular energy. It could be in private, for yourself, e.g. when you know you should be sitting down to work on a project, but the energy and ideas just won't come. It could be in public, including others, e.g. you are trying to organise a group project and various members are in disagreement about how it should be done. Get everyone to try each of the six hats on in turn.

Just for the period you are wearing it, play the role as fully as possible. You can switch hats at any time you like. Remember to try on the yellow hat before the black, or you may be so discouraged you do not want to go on. Allow the blue hat to step in if things get out of hand. It is a good idea to allow the blue hat to have the final say and sum up, even if the decision is to hand over to another hat, who will best contribute to this activity.

Exercise: INFINITE DIMENSIONS

Thanks to Burt Goldman for this exercise.[4]

Find a comfortable position, close your eyes. Breathe slowly and deeply as you relax your body and allow yourself to enter a quiet, meditative state. Imagine that you live in just one dimension among many other, infinite dimensions, and that in these other dimensions there are an infinite variety of *Yous*.

Decide which *You*, with which skills, could help you out now. It could be *You* as a public speaker, a writer, an executive.

Imagine that you are now going to enter that dimension; count from 1 to 3, and click your fingers to project yourself there.

You are now in the presence of *You*, an expert in the area of your choice. Talk to this *You*, watch *Yourself* in action and ask for advice. You can even, if invited, step inside this other *You* to try out what it feels like in that body, with those attitudes and that energy. Thank *You* for this help, and allow yourself to drift back to here and now.

Make notes of any ideas or information that came to you. It is important to write it down immediately, as this is extremely precious, personal information. You will need to think about it, experiment with it and integrate it.

You may decide to do several return trips to this same *You*, or visit another *You* in yet another dimension.

PART IV

Just Do It!

Introduction

"Knowledge without action remains ignorance."

Zen Proverb

So far, we have explored many different ideas, some profound, some light-hearted. This section will help you even more to put these ideas into practice.

First, you will see how to overcome the automatic role playing that currently makes up your sense of identity. You can now choose what roles you wish to play, based on models that represent the best and highest qualities you can imagine.

Whenever you are stuck in hard reality, the use of the magic word "IF" can come to your rescue. Magic implies changing current reality. You will be surprised to see how many respected and well-known systems – NLP, management theory, social aid – use the "As if..." Technique as a stimulus to go beyond the present.

Then comes action – physical action! Do it first, and let the feelings come later. Scientific evidence shows that this reversal of the normal order can biologically trigger the actual emotions that evade us when we just think about them.

CHAPTER 10

Role Play

*"To be a great champion, you must believe you are the best.
If you're not, pretend you are."*

Mohammed Ali

If I were to meet you for the first time and ask, "Who are you?" What would you reply? Probably your name. I might then say, "No, not your name – that's just a label your parents gave you. Who are <u>you</u>?" Then, what would you reply? Perhaps

... your nationality
... your sex (male or female)
... your colour, or race
... your profession
... your religion
... your family position
... your education
... your skills
... your titles
... your personality

Finally, you might realise that none of these is You – that sense of self that underlies all your experiences. They are all labels, or categories, with which you tend to identify, to put some sense of order into the chaos of impressions and events which make up your daily life. Life, of course, is continually spilling out of these categories, but we need them just to help organise our idea of who we are. But since no one label will fit properly, we tend to try and make our self fit the label. That is, we play a role.

When you say, "I am a teacher" or "I am a mother" or "I am an extrovert" you immediately take on the qualities of that role and act them out. You may find that you change roles many times in one day, sometimes seamlessly, sometimes with a jolt, according to how comfortably that role fits you. Where do these roles come from? Who told you what sort of person you have to be if you are a ... (fill in the blank: teacher, mother, extrovert, Johnson, etc.)

At first, as children, we pick up clues by watching others. Then we try them out by acting out different roles in our childhood games. Little by little, we develop an idea of what society expects from certain roles. We watch films, we read novels, we meet people who personify those roles and we identify with them to different extents.

During adolescence, we may feel uncomfortable about some roles that we feel have been imposed upon us. [1] Then we may rebel, rejecting that role outright and taking on another at an opposite pole. This is considered relatively normal during the troubled teens, but eventually we are expected to settle down into certain set roles when we become mature adults. In fact, for many, the role of adult means not changing roles!

Fortunately, people like you feel an inner need to keep on growing, to keep on trying out new things. You sense that stagnation is the opposite of life.

ROLE MODELS

So, you look to those who represent the brightest and the best to be your role models, to inspire and uplift you.

I think continually of those who were truly great.
Who, from the womb, remembered the soul's history
Through corridors of light where the hours are suns,
Endless and singing. Whose lovely ambition
Was that their lips, still touched with fire,
Should tell of the spirit clothed from head to foot in song.

Near the snow, near the sun, in the highest fields
See how these names are feted by the waving grass,
And by the streamers of white cloud,
And whispers of wind in the listening sky;

Role Play

The names of those who in their life fought for life,
Who wore at their hearts the fire's centre.
Born of the sun they travelled a short while towards the sun,
And left the vivid air signed with their honour.

Stephen Spender

Perhaps you realise that you have allowed the wrong role models to influence you in the past, simply because they happened to impress you at the time. And you decide that from now on, you will *choose* whom you want to emulate.

In NLP, (Neuro-Linguistic Programming) amongst other systems, this is called modelling. You are encouraged to choose people who represent the top of their profession or sport, and to study what it is about them that works – what strategies they use that you could apply to your own life.

The field of sport is an obvious example. Young people in training will attend every match of their top role model. They will spend hours studying films and videos to observe the slightest change in posture, or flick of the wrist, which makes the difference, which makes them a champion! They will devour every book and article about their hero to find out not only what he/she does, but also how he/she thinks and feels – what motivates him, what makes her tick. And then, bit-by-bit, the trainees will experiment themselves, knowing that every champion has reached his position by climbing on the shoulders of those champions who went before. And, of course, even the tens of thousands of spectators, who have no intention of playing the sport themselves, will still imitate their admired role model, even if it is just adopting the same T-shirt or haircut.

The same applies to business. The self-made millionaires, the top CEOs are studied and interviewed to find the secrets of their success. The market is flooded with books and magazines telling you how you, too, can do it! The recent practice of finding a mentor in one's chosen profession gives aspiring young people the chance not only to be guided by their role model's advice and know-how, but also to emulate their special personal energy.

In every field of art, be it painting, sculpture, writing or especially the performing arts – singing, dancing, acting, playing music – we aspire to be like our role models. For those studying in the same field, this may mean observing and imitating their technical skills. For the admiring members of the public it means cutting out articles, sticking up posters, buying the same clothes, adopting the same manner of walking and talking, in short, doing everything possible to be like their adored star. The role model becomes an idol.

In our culture, just being famous can inspire this desire to emulate. "I want to be like Madonna! I want to be like Beckham!" Celebrities come under exceptionally harsh criticism for unsocial or immoral behaviour because we all recognise their power to influence the young and impressionable. We do not want *that sort of person* as a role model for the current generation.

Social and political figureheads, people exhibiting expertise or genius in their field, and great spiritual leaders (Mahatma Gandhi, the Dalai Lama, Mother Teresa) are all available as role models. Whom have *you* chosen, consciously or unconsciously?

At the end of this chapter is an exercise to help you identify which role models can help you in certain fields and how to integrate their desirable traits into your personality.

WE ALL ROLE PLAY

For the human being, role playing is as natural as breathing and walking. It is how we learn, experiment and discard, and keep on growing. If a role suits us, we can keep it and make it our own. If not, we can easily discard it, especially if it is plain to all concerned that it was not *really* us – we were just playing around!

"People do not mind playing the fool so long as it is quite clear that they are just playing a role. They even take pride in putting on a good performance and playing an extremely foolish fool. That now becomes a measure of achievement and excellence. The role has taken over and the ego is now stage director.

To play at being someone else allows the ego to go beyond its normal restrictive self-image... A role gives freedom. Given a well-defined role we can act out (difficult) parts with pleasure in our acting skills rather than damage to our egos. Without the protection of a formal role, the ego is at risk." [2]

Edward de Bono uses this human tendency to play roles as a deliberate and conscious device to develop and balance different thinking styles. *(See chapter 9)*

ROLES BORN OF NECESSITY

Most of us find that society forces certain roles on us. We may find some of them conflicting and have to spend time and energy juggling the different roles, trying to balance them.

Fortunately, we are not often lead to the extremes of Preethi Nair, fledgling author, who found herself having to play two different lives to cope with others' expectations. Her story is told in *The Evening Standard*, 14/9/00, under the headline: WRITER LIVED DOUBLE LIFE AS A PR PLUGGING HER OWN NOVEL.

Struggling as a new, unknown writer to get her first book accepted by publishers, she came up with the idea of being her own publicist.

Secretly re-inventing herself, she posed as public relations executive Pru Menon, and began a double life promoting the work of hot new author Preethi Nair. The multi-national PR firm Creative House was born in her back bedroom.

"I got two of everything, telephones with different ringing tones and separate e-mails for Pru and myself. I lowered my voice two octaves when callers want to speak to me as Preethi. I decided to go it alone because nobody can put the same passion into promoting my book that I can, because nobody believes in it as I do. She's the total opposite of sentimental, wimpy me. She can handle rejection better than me."

The situation at times became almost farcical, at one stage having to pass the phone from one to the other, but it worked. Preetha's novel is on several best-seller lists, and she admits to being very much indebted to her alter ego.

THE WRONG ROLE

How often have you found yourself unhappy with certain aspects of your personality, but unable to do anything about it? "I'm lazy – I'm disorganised – I'm boring – I'm fat!" You eventually gave up even trying to alter the situation because you thought, "That's me. That's just the way I am." Please, no more!

I hope by now you understand that that *me*, the self you complain of, is no more than a role you have over-identified with. There is no need to ever be stuck in a role you don't like.

If you are living and behaving in ways that are no longer appropriate, you have started to believe that your self-image is actually you.

Change the image, and you will change the behaviour.

A smoker, for example, may believe that he could never stop smoking without feeling stressed, deprived, lacking in confidence. He is afraid of changing his role – from smoker to non-smoker. Rather than making a voluntary effort to change his behaviour (stop smoking), he will do far better to train himself mentally, so that first, he is able to *imagine* himself in his new role as a non-smoker. The more he can build up this new image of himself as a non-smoker, with all the wonderful, positive benefits he can think of, the more easily he can accept that this is his new role. If he can see himself calm, serene, confident, enjoying great new health and energy, being more attractive and agreeable, the battle is won before it has started. In fact, there is no battle. It feels natural and easy to behave according to your own self-image. I cannot say too often, "Change the image, and you change the behaviour."

The German-born philosopher Walter Kaufmann taught this. He saw people building a prison of their own emotions, then unable to change because they believed they could not. His method was one of questioning: first asking yourself if you would be better off otherwise, and how. "Think of alternatives, using your imagination."

MENTAL REHEARSAL

Since the human potential movement first started to flourish in the 1960's, I have come across the important of self-image again and again, in various books, workshops and seminars. The techniques that really help, like the ones you will find at the end of the chapter, are those in which you plunge right into feeling and experimenting the new role as a sort of mental rehearsal. You visualise in detail, movement and colour all the different elements of the new role you want to play, imagining you are *already* in the situation, seeing, hearing, smelling, tasting, touching – making it as vivid and as real as possible.

This is quite different from a fantasy. What you are doing is preparing your mind to accept the desired role, acting in your imagination as if you have already acquired the new capabilities. You are creating *expectancy*.

"If you want to be successful in a new job or a new relationship or almost any aspect of life, you need to have positive expectations for the future." That's the word from New York University and University of Hamburg researchers who determined that positive expectations lead to success, while those who just fantasize about the future rarely have those dreams come true.[3]

Imagining yourself already in the role is also quite different from *wanting* it to happen. As long as you go on *wanting* it, you haven't got it! Wanting implies a separation from what is wanted, and psychologically creates a block to actually achieving it. All the efforts of your limited willpower will be in vain. As our friend Emile Coué said so long ago, "When imagination and willpower are in conflict, it is always imagination that will win."

When you consciously choose what role you would like to play, and bring all the power of your imagination to work on it, you are creating a fire within which will motivate your mind and energise your body, working at very deep levels. A mind which has already been primed by Mental Rehearsal of the desired role or situation will be open and receptive to normally imperceptible clues in the environment that will provide useful information for achieving the goal. A body which has memorised the movements and actions performed in mental rehearsal will respond by reactivating the same circuits and achieving levels of performance never before achieved. Recent studies in neurophysiology demonstrate that the same brain structures are activated whether we perform a movement or simply think about it.

Just one example: physical reaction time has been shown to be affected by imagining oneself in another role. In this ingenious experiment, "participants were randomly assigned to one of two groups. People in one group were asked to press a switch the moment that a light came on. They were asked to try as hard as they could. The other group was told to imagine that they were fighter pilots with very fast reactions. They were then given exactly the same task as the first group, that is, to press a button whenever a light was illuminated. Amazingly, people in the second group responded much faster than those in the first group. They expected to do well and their expectations affected their behaviour." [4]

Mental rehearsal gives you control over your own expectancy. Have you ever been to a medium when you were feeling down, to be told that fortune would smile on you, things would get better, and your love life, health and job were moving into a new positive, successful period. Your spirits lift, you attack life anew, and lo and behold, the medium was right! You have made the prediction come true - it was a self-fulfilling prophecy. You know this is possible, so why not be your own medium; predict and create your own future, as you want it to be, and build your positive expectancy in mental rehearsal.

One of my professional colleagues in Paris, when I mentioned in passing that I was writing this book, pressed me to describe further what it was about. After just a few sentences of explanation, her eyes widened. She became very enthusiastic. It seems she was able to completely transform her own life by pretending to be someone else – and finally becoming that person in reality. She was so dedicated to playing her new role that she even imagined the director, the film studio, and the cameras upon her! I will let her tell her story in her own words...

ROBERTA'S STORY

So, Roberta, you actually found that role playing helped you change areas of your life?

Yes. I had two amazing experiences.

The first one was when I was eleven years old. I looked at myself and I said, "I am full of complexes." I felt I was ugly, I was too shy, I didn't have friends, nobody liked me, I had a lot of blockages, ... a lot of things. And I said, "I don't like myself. But how can I change?" So I looked at children around me in school who were popular. And I said, "What do they do to be popular?" So I observed their behaviour, and then I started to say, "I'm going to play a role. I'm going to do it!"

The trouble was that people already knew me from what I was. I had been defined. So when I started to play a role, they always said, "You look funny. What's wrong with you?"

So I managed to get my parents to change me to another school. I said, "When I go into that school, I'm going to play a role of what I would like to be." So I changed everything – the way I dressed, the way I spoke, the way I acted, and I tried to imitate everybody that I felt was the way I wanted to be.

And I did. And everything changed. Everything! People acted toward me like nobody had ever acted before – teachers, friends. I had plenty of friends, everybody was wanting to be with me, teachers were taking me as an example, everything changed. I felt happier, I felt... people started telling me I was beautiful, and as a consequence, then I felt, "But still it's not me. I'm lying."

Ahhh. That's just what I was going to ask you. Did you feel that this was becoming real or not?

Yes. I said, "But this is not me, and it's fake... and I love it! So I continued. I said, Well, let's play this game for as long as I can. And eventually I realised that I was feeling better, and that things started to become what they were, and they became my new Me.

And one day, it was really something, because a friend of my mother's that I hadn't seen in two years, she came home, she saw me and she said, "Wow, what happened to Roberta? She's transformed. She's not the same." And that really did it. That was the first time.

Then...

Hang on a minute... This was at eleven?

Yes.

So at eleven years old you had quite an awareness for a child. In your own childish language, did you call it playing a role? Or how did you express it to yourself? I'm going to...?

Yes, play a role. I loved playing a role. For example I said I'm going to be an actress.

OK. So I'm going to be an actress playing this role, and I'll pretend I'm them.

That's very conscious.

Yes, and I even played thinking that I had cameras. I felt that there were cameras on me, and I felt very important. I thought, Wow, I'm the star of the movie and I'm playing a role. I always have to look completely perfect and do the things that the film producer is telling me to, so really I had always a picture of these cameras following me everywhere, sometimes even in the street. I felt as if someone was following me.

And this was all your own idea? You stumbled on this when you thought, I don't like me, but that's the sort of person I want to be?

Absolutely.

I said, I don't like me – why am I like this, and what could I do to change, and why are other people so successful, or like I would like to be?

I didn't really ask, Why am I not? I asked, How can I be?

So this was the first time, and when I saw what happened I said, Wow!

Then something more or less bad happened. We moved to another country, we went to Brazil, from Italy, and I had a lot of difficulties. I arrived there, and when I felt that I was going to a new school again, and would play a role again, it wouldn't work, because the people there were completely different. I had a culture shock. So my role play was completely absurd in the circumstances. So I had a very deep depression that lasted about two years, and I was just in pain. The people there, the people I met, I didn't want to be like them. So it demotivated me completely from doing anything.

So again, I went back into my self-analysis, and at this stage I was seventeen years old, and exactly the same thing happened. I actually had to drop out of school, because it was becoming really bad. I mean, I was fainting, going to school. They were so different from me, people were so different from me – I was in pain and I couldn't stand it. My mother had been so ill that she had almost died, and I had big quarrels with my brother and with my father. I was in a mess, a real mess. Actually, I was anorexic, and the doctor said, if she doesn't do something, she might die.

And that did it. I said, I don't want to die! But I'm in such pain. So, I remembered that. And I did two things.

The first one was la méthode Coué. I didn't know it then, I had never heard about it. I just said, I'm going to start telling myself, "I'm happy, I'm happy, I'm happy." And I spent every single second of my day repeating to myself, "I'm happy, I'm happy, I'm happy." Even as I was crying... "I'm happy, I'm happy. I'm happy". In about a month's time I made new friends (I had stopped going to school, I had been in high school.) And this friend of mine said, Why are you not going to school? I know a school that is really nice, maybe you could go there. I said, But I don't like school. And he said, But it's an international school, I think you would like it. People are more like you, they're not like Brazilians, who were different from me. I enquired, I went, and eventually I enrolled, not without difficulties from my parents, but eventually I enrolled. And when I enrolled I said, "Now I'm going to go in there, and I'm going to be the new person I want to be, in an international context. Because people kept telling me that I looked sad, that I was not fun to be with, and I said I'm going to be fun to be with. So I changed my clothes again, because I was in jeans; I bought myself dresses, nice clothes, made my hair beautiful. I went there on the first day, and I smiled, and when I introduced myself to everybody I said, I've done this, and that, and I'm happy and I want to travel the world, and I started to say only positive things, and to be very happy, and to smile, and smile and smile.

Even though you didn't feel it inside?

Yeah, I didn't feel it at all. Oh no. I was even feeling very bad. But I kept faking and faking. Again, the cameras were on me and I looked at how the style of the school was, and I tried to see what would make someone successful here, popular. So I observed all that and I started to do it, and that was in that case to be musically orientated, so I started to play piano. You had to be very friendly, you had to help people, you had to laugh a lot and be funny, so I started to do all of that. And actually, in two months time, one boy in the class fell in love with me and that was my first boyfriend.

Were you still feeling, Oh, he doesn't like the real me, he likes the person I'm pretending to be? Or by then was it starting to be real?

Actually, by the time he got interested in me, then it started to be real. I actually believed it. And then I said, But this is what I want to be, so this is what I am, and let's continue, and then I felt completely comfortable.

O.K. This is what I want to be, so this is what I am. Wow!

And people started to tell me what I was.

Right!

And I liked it. You're beautiful, you're fun to be with, you're great, you're smart, you're all these things, and I said, Yeah, that's what I want to be, but if they're telling me, I must be, because you cannot fake something like that, after all, so now I had become it.

This time, however, it was for the rest of my life. Since then I had highs and lows, or ups and downs, but ever since I've been able not to play a role any more, but to be myself as I really am.

That is exactly what I am writing about!

When I heard you were writing this book, I said, Hey, I had this experience!

That is a brilliant case study. Maybe I should be talking about this more – maybe lots of people, somewhere in their lives, have made that decision, and don't talk about it because they feel it's cheating, or it's faking.

Not long ago I read an article about one of these self-development courses, that you can play a role to actually develop the behaviour you want to have, but there is not an entire book about it.

The title is to be "The Magic of Make Believe"

and the sub-title, "How to Give the Performance of Your Life!"

As a psychologist AND an actress, I think I'm the person to write the book! I know what it's like to have to study to play a role, and to make it real.

And you have some movies where actors went so much into the role, they said that in their real life, it overflowed.

And it goes with the method, where you keep telling yourself, "I am, I am," and then it starts happening.

But a lot of people stop themselves. "I am – but I'm not really. I am – but I'm not really." They say, "Well, I can't ACT happy, if I'm not REALLY happy" and they try and start from the inside out. And, of course, they never feel happy, so they never finish up acting happy, and nothing ever happens.

Everybody knows that it's a physiological truth that if you smile, it actually creates endorphines, and you actually start to feel happier. And that's from the outside in.

Thank you, Roberta.

Exercises

Exercise: MENTAL REHEARSAL, no. 2

This can be used for a variety of situations, when you feel stuck in your present role. First of all, be very clear and precise about the mental image you wish to create.

If you are feeling sluggish and slobby, and want to be more healthy, create a picture of yourself playing a particular sport, or jogging, or some other healthy activity. Decide on your weight and measurements. Picture the clothes you are wearing. The important thing is to really get a *feel* of being this person. An effective way to do this is to create the picture of the new *You* in a full-length mirror, and then, like Alice, step into the mirror, and step into the body you have pictured. Use all of your senses to stimulate your imagination – sight, hearing, smell, taste and touch. Feel yourself moving around as this new you; experience the body sensations and especially the emotions – pride, confidence, energy, pleasure, self-assurance, satisfaction and enjoyment! Taste the rewards in advance. Your brain will register this as a desirable outcome and tune in your mind and body to do everything to achieve it!

If you are feeling doubtful of your capacities, and want to be more self-confident, choose a very specific situation, like speaking in public, or making a presentation, and experience yourself in your new role, with all the qualities you desire.

If you know from past experience that you always collapse in a stammering heap when a superior criticises your work, break the pattern by rehearsing mentally how you would like to react – with poise and grace, listening attentively, explaining calmly the difficulties, and asserting yourself without being defensive. Repeat this regularly until it seems to be natural for you.

If you consider that you are messy and lack order in your life, and would like to be more organised, picture yourself in very specific situations, tidying your desk, arriving on time, finding immediately everything you have filed away safely. Identify with the sense of satisfaction that comes from being an organised person. You will find that you no longer have to force yourself to be tidy. It will be automatic: "Oh, but a person as organised as I am always tidies up before leaving."

There is no end to the possibilities. So long as you can imagine yourself in a new role, you can rehearse it in your imagination. The trick is to pre-live the situation, so you know in advance what it is like, and it feels more like the norm than your old self-image.

In all these situations, keep the new image in mind throughout the day, whenever you think of the situation, whenever a related incident comes up. Don't allow yourself to slip back into the old habits of thinking. Remember how *good* it felt when you rehearsed it. Anticipate how good it *will* feel when you have a chance to act it out in life.

Exercise: ON STAGE!

This is very similar to the previous exercise, but adapted for certain cases where you cannot even imagine yourself in a different role. Your goal seems so remote from your past experience that you have no point of reference.

This is where you can use the image of another person who has already achieved the goal. Choose as a role model a person who is already expert in the chosen field. Someone who finds it easy, natural and pleasurable to engage in the desired behaviour – a person you admire, or respect, and would like to emulate.

Now, you will imagine three scenes being played out on a stage.

In the first scene, you will be in the audience, observing your model play out the part that you want to play out in your life. He, of course, performs it to perfection. Study his gestures, his stance, his voice, his actions, as if you are understudying the star of the play, ready to take over his part.

In the second scene, you will again be in the audience, watching the same scene being played, but this time you see yourself on stage. You have taken over the part. Watch how you use the same gestures, stance, voice and actions of the star that you have studied. Follow the scene through to its conclusion.

In the third scene, the action is repeated as before, but you are no longer a spectator. You merge with the role completely. What you have observed, you now act out, seeing through your eyes, hearing through your ears. Now it is *you* who is performing the gestures, stance, voice and actions. It becomes a personal experience.

Use this technique for any situation that seems so far removed from you, or your current self-image, that you are unable to identify with it. The role model provides the intermediary step and frees up your imagination.

CHAPTER 11

The Magic Word "If"

"Live as if you were to die tomorrow,
Learn as if you were to live for ever."

Mahandas Gandhi

Let me start with a personal story of when the "if" word flipped my mind like a pancake and gave me a breakthrough.

From what my parents had told me, I knew that at three years old I had made up two imaginary playmates, Gillie and Carrie. Apparently I would push them for hours on the swing, and squeal if an adult went to sit down on the same chair. But for me, today, this was just hearsay. I had no conscious recollection of them at all.

Then, when I was doing my hypnotism training, a volunteer was required for a demonstration of an age-regression technique to remember a forgotten childhood event. This seemed a wonderful opportunity to satisfy my curiosity – just what were they like?

The trainer, Dr. Richard Harte, took me back to three years old using the Calendar Technique. It worked just fine, and I found myself in the kitchen of my childhood home, with facial and vocal expressions of a 3-year old, with vivid impressions of the furniture, my clothes, everything – except Gillie and Carrie! I was led to a moment when they were there with me, and asked, "What do they look like?"

I don't know," I replied, and felt a huge wave of disappointment sweep over me. While my adult thought, "It's not going to happen", my child's bottom lip quivered. "I can't see them – they're invisible."

Dr. Harte was not phased at all. He uttered the magic word: *"IF* you could see them, or imagine what they looked like, how would that be?"

That was all that was needed. Suddenly the memory of how I imagined them leapt into full consciousness – and I started to laugh!

They were so funny, and happy, and delightful, and I was so pleased to see them again! (I have a tape of the experience, and I am actually guffawing so much that I can't speak, and Dr. Harte has to calm me.)

The words came tumbling out – pointed pixie ears, huge grins from ear to ear, a boy and a girl, twins, my height, dressed in "fairy stuff". They would accompany me for hours of solitary play in the back garden while my parents were busy with my newborn sister, plunging into the deep fishpond and bringing back stories of magical underwater adventures.

It was truly one of the best presents I have ever had, thanks to Dr. Harte and his judicious use of the word "if".

MAGIC

I call "if" the magic word, because it allows us to forget, temporarily, the limitations imposed by reality, and to explore how the impossible could become possible. Magic lifts us up, frees us and empowers us. And the magic of "if" is at the heart of Make Believe.

I receive regularly in my e-mails a variation of these words, which obviously strike a chord in thousands of people:

"Work *as if* you don't need the money

Dance *as if* no one is looking

Love *as if* you have never been hurt."

In other words, don't allow yourself to sink too deep in the quagmire we call reality, which is too often a set of limiting beliefs in itself.

THE METHOD

Constantin Stanislavsky, the famous teacher/director for the Moscow Arts Company, regularly used the magic "IF" in his classes and rehearsals.

In "An Actor Prepares", he introduces his techniques to the world through the mock diary of a young actor, Kostya, who describes his progress through a series of exercises presented by the instructor, Tortsov, (Stanislavsky in disguise). Gradually he learns to develop and trust in his own mental and emotional resources.

One of the techniques which helps him is the magic "IF". Especially when called to play a difficult emotion or an alien experience, the actor begins his work asking, "What would I feel like (or what would I do) IF I were in these circumstances?"

A simple word, and a simple question, it is the springboard to boundless creativity and inspiration. It allows the actor to accept that he is playing a fiction, and to go beyond it, granting him permission to believe in his role, in the same way that a little girl believes that her doll is real, or a little boy believes he is Superman.

This book inspired the famous Method school of acting, and laid the groundwork for much of the great acting over the next century.

This is a useful little habit that you could develop in your daily life. Ask yourself, 'How would I act IF I felt more confident?', or, 'What would I do IF I had lots of experience in this situation?'

NLP AND LANGUAGE

Neuro-Linguistic Programming recognises the magical power of language to transform our perception of reality, and even refers to 'magic' in its book titles. [1]

Since what we perceive of external reality is filtered through our attitudes, beliefs, habits, emotions, etc. our perception is *never* the same as reality – just a representation that helps us make sense of it. "The map is not the territory."

When we change our perception, it seems as if we are changing reality, and therein lies the magic!

NLP and other related methods use many variations of the word "if" to bring about this change.

Attributing Sensory Qualities
– *If* you could give a shape, a colour, and a size to your fear,
(or anxiety, or pain) what would it look like?
– *If* it made a noise, what would it sound like?
– *If* your fear had a texture, what would it feel like?
And so on, with smell and taste. Once the problem can be
described in words as something tangible, (even though symbolic),
it can be consciously manipulated until no longer damaging.

Try this with children – they love it!

Overcoming Resistance
- "Sorry, it's just not possible!"
- "*If* it were possible, *what would it take* to do it?"
  This is a really neat way of sidestepping the argument of whether it is possible or not, and prompting the person to use his imagination creatively. I've used it very successfully to help a stalled client in hypnosis.
- "I can't see anything. It's all dark."
- "If you could see something, what would it take to be clearer?"
  Or,
- "I just can't stop smoking. I can't resist cigarettes."
- "If you could resist a cigarette, what would it take?"
  Please, do try this with obstinate public servants or administrators. It works wonders! No guarantees, of course, but…
- "Sorry, we're completely booked."
- "If it were possible to squeeze me in, what would it take to do it?"

They are momentarily thrown off track (the 'No' track) while they are asking themselves, in effect, how to get round the problem.

What if…?
This is very similar to the above, and is particularly useful to ask when someone is stuck in a belief-limiting pattern. For example:
- "I can't trust people."
- "What would happen IF you trusted people?"

The person is encouraged to describe this previously unimagined possibility in as much sensory detail as she can, until she has a clear, fully focused image. The more different avenues are explored through the "if", the more the person realises she actually has a rich set of choices available.

Other variations:
- "I have to behave respectfully to my superiors."
- "What would happen if you failed to act respectfully?"

Or,
- "I mustn't get too deeply involved."
- "What would happen if you got deeply involved?"
  Or,
- "No one can do that!"
- "What if you could?"

THE "AS IF" TECHNIQUE

"As if" thinking is just a sophisticated name for pretending. It is a technique used in encouraging creativity, problem solving, therapy, improving skills and business planning – and it's also fun!

It is one of the most direct ways to get around a limitation – simply pretend you have gotten round it. If you want something you don't have, the easiest way of getting there is to pretend you now have it, and then act AS IF it were true.

Creativity

To stimulate creativity and right-brain thinking, you can act as if you are an inspired creative genius in your field, and you have a nonstop flow of new ideas. Or, you can pretend you are having a conversation with an imaginary mentor. Write ideas in a notebook, as if your mentor is replying to your questions. Or, you can write yourself a letter of encouragement, as if you are another person, wiser and more experienced, who has been watching the real you struggling with your difficulties.

Problem-solving

Imagine you can time-travel to the desired future, where you have already solved your problem. It is AS IF you are now enjoying the fruits of your success, relaxed and free from the stress, the obligation of solving the problem. From this future viewpoint, you can now look back and see how you got there. You can actually get extremely useful insights like this.

Improving Skills

Again, you can play "as if" with the future, so that your goals become more specific and real. Picture yourself as if you have already achieved the standard you wish in your field of sport, or with a musical instrument, or whatever. Now ask yourself, "How is this for me? What do I see...? What do I hear...? What do I feel...? The clearer your goal, the easier to connect with it and move towards it.

Social Work

Barbara Sher describes how she used "as if" to work with ex-addicts. [2] Since it took too long to build up a new self-image, she got them to "act as if" – to dress *as if* they respected themselves, to act *as if* they deserved to get the job, to work *as if* they were first rate – whether it was true or not. Soon they were accomplishing marvels and taking their place in society.

"It worked," says Barbara, "because high self-esteem comes *after* action, not before. "Do it first, learn it second," one of them said to me... Action will raise your self-esteem better than affirmations. Telling yourself you're a good person doesn't last for long... Acting as if works better than any kind of thinking, because when you've *done something* you feel proud of yourself."

Therapy

When a client is having difficulty achieving something, or even imagining she can achieve it, the therapist does not need to insist that she make an effort to do so. He need only suggest she act as if she were responding appropriately. Little does she know that it comes down to exactly the same thing!

"In terms of the outcome, where the act ends and the reality begins is ambiguous since the responses are identical. Suggesting that a client act "as if" he or she is comfortable, relaxed, ... or whatever, paves the way for the client to really experience those suggestions without any personal demands being made." [3]

Finally, does it really matter so much if it is real or pretence, provided the result is achieved?

The As If technique can help the therapist as well as the client. Confronted with a disease, for example, which has resisted all attempts of standard medical treatment, and which may or may not have a psychosomatic basis, it is actually more helpful to act on the assumption that it is, indeed, psychosomatic. By acting *as if* this is true, the therapist will be able to behave more congruently, his own belief will stimulate the belief of his client, and in many cases healing or change will be achieved, even if it is only the placebo effect! The important thing is that positive change is achieved.

"You can talk about it as if the people were *pretending* to be changed, but as long as they pretend effectively for the rest of their life, I'm satisfied. That's real enough for me." [4]

"As if" is often used in hypnotherapy, where the client in the hypnotic state is much less likely to reject a suggestion because it seems unlikely or illogical. Using "trance logic", he no longer needs his experience to be entirely realistic or rational, and can temporarily accept new suggested realities.

"The opportunity for the client to respond as if something were real can be a gateway to deeper feelings and issues appropriate for the therapeutic intervention." [5]

Business Applications

It is recommended in much professional training, that if you want to obtain a certain promotion, or polish your professional image, you should act as if you are already there. You will train yourself – and others – to see you in a new light. When you behave like the professional you want to be, you will dress for success, project an image of confidence and competence, and automatically command respect from your peers and employers. If you're serious about getting ahead, then act serious!

Future planning in any company involves imagining what the future might be like IF certain things happen. This includes a fair bit of guesswork. A more effective approach is to pretend you are sitting in your office five years in the future, after five years of success, and ask yourself, "What did we do to get here?"

"This small shift in perspective can produce amazing information. You act AS IF you are in the future. See, hear and feel your success. Then look back to find out how you achieve your desired state." [6]

The AS IF technique can also be extremely useful in helping to get a customer thinking about a desired future, thus concluding a deal.

"Both future planning and the conditional close have a strong element of "Let's Pretend". In the conditional close, you pretend you can satisfy one or more needs of your customer. You ask, "*If* we can do A, *then* will you be happy to do B?"

For example, "*If* we can arrange for you to talk to some of our satisfied customers, *then* you'd feel good about signing an agreement with us?"

or again, "*If* they give us good marks, *then* we can set up dates. Which month would be best for you?" [7]

BEYOND VISUALISATION

I have come across certain worldly settings where visualisation is rejected out-of-hand as New Age – implying that it is just self-indulgent fantasizing with no connection with hard-core reality or real results. In fact, visualisation is an extremely powerful technique with proven results in medicine and health, sports, professional and personal development.

You no doubt have already experimented with many different visualisation techniques and, in fact, most of the exercises in this book have some basis in visualisation.

So why does it not always work? I am convinced that it is the AS IF factor that makes all the difference. Visualising the desired goal is all well and good, but you need to have the impression that you are already there, living the experience as if it is real. By concentrating on details and rich sensory experience you can create an inner reality. This is the first step to manifesting your goal as an outer reality.

The next step, which is often the missing link in visualisation exercises, is to *act* in daily life, *as if* the goal is already achieved, as if you are already the person you want to be. This creates an attitude of expectancy that will continue to work at many deeper levels of your consciousness.

"You must not wait to act until you have proof – you must act as if it is there, and it will come through. 'Do the thing and you will have the power,' said Emerson." [8]

Don't worry if your critical mind intervenes to object, "But you're just pretending!" Talk back to it – "That's right, I am! And isn't it fun!" Act as if it's true, expect it to happen, and you create the optimal conditions for it to come about. By dint of repetition, AS IF becomes AS IS. More of this in the next chapter...

Two thousand years ago, one of the greatest psychologists who ever lived advised us to pray AS IF our prayer has ALREADY been answered.

"Therefore I say unto you, What things so ever ye desire, when ye pray, believe that ye receive them, and ye shall have them."

(Mark 11:24)

"We can act AS IF there was a God; feel AS IF we were free; consider Nature AS IF she were full of special designs; lay plans AS IF we were to be immortal; and we find then that these words do make a genuine difference in our moral life."

William James

Exercises

Exercise: START SMALL

What would you like to change TODAY?

Ask yourself, "What would it be like IF I were nice to my boss?" or, "What IF I ate only fruit today?" or, "IF I were really efficient and organised today, how would it feel?" or simply, "IF I were to arrive 10 minutes early, what would it take?"

Don't alarm yourself or set off your defence mechanisms by telling yourself you *have* to do it! Just wonder IF...

Then think about how it might happen. Enjoy yourself. Have fun with what comes up.

Then, do it!

Act as if it is something totally normal and natural for you to do this, and you may be surprised that it is easier than you think! By biting off a little chunk at a time, you will gradually achieve big results.

Exercise: IF I WERE ALREADY...

Pick any situation in your life that seems heavy, blocked, stagnant, resistant to change. Now, pretend that the problems have all been solved some time ago, and you are *already* in a wonderful new situation.

If that were so, what would it be like? Imagine specifically how it would be, in lots of sensory detail. What can you hear, see, smell and touch? What body sensations do you feel, what emotions, AS IF you are already living this future result.

Then, look back at all the events in between.

How did you get here? What did you do?

Write down any ideas, without criticising or condemning.

Looking backward often triggers more resources than the As If technique looking forward.

Somehow if we can just kid ourselves (pretend!) that we have been there, done that, the pressure to perform just evaporates.

CHAPTER 12

Action!

"Fake it till you make it!"

How brash, and how American! It almost makes you wince; it is so simplistic and so arrogant. Yet… it contains the very *essence* of the value of pretending. Go through the actions, physically, even if you don't believe just yet that you are doing it for real (yes, you are faking it!) and sooner or later, you will find that the emotional processes and thought patterns will actually follow the promptings of your body.

So, if you are stuck in the quandary of wondering if you are capable, stop thinking and just do! Act! Start performing the gestures, movements and activities you may have already started visualising. It's quite true that wishing won't make it so, but *doing* will!

The mind-body mechanism is not a one-way street. If your mind is hesitating, not ready to give instructions to your body, then put your body through the necessary motions and let it feed instructions to your mind.

Yes, it feels strange at first. And since the mind is used to playing the boss, it feels uncomfortable and protests, "This is fake!" However, if the body persists in this new behaviour until it becomes familiar, then even habitual, the mind accepts it as normal and provides the corresponding belief.

EVERYDAY OBSERVATIONS

Laymen often call this effect, the tail wagging the dog. We have all had moments such as when a friend happens to call by when we are feeling in a low mood. Rather than contaminate our friend, we will put on a happy face, acting as if we're in a good mood, smiling, laughing, chatting, until, before we realise it, we actually do feel happier. We have reversed the usual process, but it is no less real for that.

As William James says, "Does a person smile because he is happy, or is he happy because he smiles?"

Or again, if we find ourselves in an intimidating situation where we do not want others to know we are afraid, putting on a brave face, throwing the shoulders back and speaking firmly can have the immediate effect of increasing our confidence.

As the popular song from *The King and I* goes:

Whenever I feel afraid
I hold myself erect
And whistle a happy tune
So no one will suspect
I'm afraid.
The result of this deception
Is very strange to tell
Whenever I fool the people I meet
I fool myself as well!
I whistle a happy tune
And every single time
The happiness in the tune
Convinces me that I'm
Not afraid.
Make believe you're brave
And the trick will take you far
You may be as brave
As you make believe you are.

So, if you can just encourage yourself to accomplish that first step by going through the motions, the rest will follow. And the final performance will be identical to that which requires real belief.

"Throw yourself into that pose (Rodin's *The Thinker*) – physically not mentally – and you will become a thinker. Why? Because if you playact being a thinker, you will become one. Go through the motions... even if you do not feel emotionally involved. In time your emotions will catch up with your motions... Please note that intention is not enough. You must *go through the motions*; the surprising thing is that on a physiological level it might actually work. Signals become reality. The mask is followed by the substance."[1]

OBJECTION OVERRULED — (PHYSICAL LIMITS)

Another objection that could be raised against physically acting out the desired behaviour is that we have certain physical limits that cannot be ignored, which will become only too apparent if we attempt to act otherwise. Yet, perhaps not so much after all...

It is well known that, following hypnotic suggestions that they are very strong, subjects are capable of amazing feats of physical strength of which, under normal conditions they would not be capable. Since one can obviously not pretend to do something physically impossible, that strength must have been already there! By acting as if he is a champion weight lifter or strong man, the subject actually releases a potential he already had within him, but which has been held back because he believes he is smaller, weaker or more helpless than he actually is. The psychologist F.M.H. Myers explained that the talents and abilities displayed by hypnotic subjects were due to a purgation of memory of past failures. So hypnosis does not *add* anything to one's actual strength – but it does overcome a negative idea that had previously been preventing him from expressing his full strength.

Remember the experiment where subjects increased their physical reaction time because they were making believe they were fighter pilots?

In the same way, all sorts of other unsuspected strengths or powers can be released (including in the waking state) by ignoring past failures and criticisms and acting *as if it were impossible to fail*.

It is often tempting to blame lack of success on a physical failing: "Since I'm big-boned, I can't be a ballet dancer" or "Since I've got a big nose, no one will find me attractive," when, in fact, the real problem – and solution – lies in self-image.

One of my colleagues in hypnotherapy recounts how a young ballerina came to him with a weight problem. "I'm already quite tall", she complained, "but unless I lose some weight I'll never get out of the *corps de ballet*. Everyone calls me fatso." My colleague gave her a first session, which he recorded, in which he gave her only ego-strengthening suggestions, to boost her self-esteem and confidence. There was no mention of weight. Since she was about to leave on tour and could not come back for a couple of months, he gave her the cassette and told her to listen to it regularly before she went to sleep. She called some months later to say she wouldn't need any more sessions after all.

"So, you lost some weight then?"

"Well, not really that much. But it doesn't seem to matter any more. I have a lead role in the next production. My dancing has improved so much that no one seems to notice my weight."

But if one were cursed with a large nose and cross-eyes, for example, would it really help to just act as if one were beautiful? It seemed to work for Barbara Streisand, who flaunted her magnificent profile in the flamboyant guise of Nefertiti, and other great beauties of history. And as any plastic surgeon will tell you, what is behind the face is more important than what is in front. Maxwell Maltz, who wrote the classic self-help book on *Psycho-Cybernetics* [2] was himself a plastic surgeon who was struck by the importance of self-image as distinct from actual body appearance. Although most of his patients were happy when their facial defects or deformities were improved, some, he noted, could not accept that they looked any different. They still saw themselves as ugly or disfigured, and no amount of proof would convince them otherwise. What they needed was surgery on their self-image, or an emotional face lift. So, do not fall back on excuses. It's too easy to deny yourself a bright future.

ACTING A ROLE

Don't renounce a better role in life by insisting that to be real you must start from within. You know already that it is possible to influence your emotions from the outside in. You can boost that inner self-image by spending a little extra time on your external appearance, checking on your hairdo, makeup, clothes, as well as adopting the posture which goes with being at your best.

Similarly, when you are wearing old jeans and sloppy T-shirt, and you allow your body to slump and sag, you feel lacking energy and lazy.

For the actor, this is called the external approach. He will begin by studying how others project emotions.

"For instance, one expresses anger by raising the volume and intensity of the voice and tightening one's face muscles. The actor will apply these external signs on himself. Performers think of this as putting on a mask. The teacher who finds it difficult to maintain discipline might use the mask of a disciplinarian to bring about order. Actors will tell you that the external will frequently lead to the internal." [3]

Sir Laurence Olivier, considered one of the greatest actors of the 20th century, habitually approached a new role from the exterior. He would spend many hours in front of the mirror, experimenting with wigs, make-up and prostheses, until he had just the right nose, eyebrows or moustache that seemed to suit his character. He needed first to see the character in the mirror before he could start to inhabit him. Then, different body positions, gestures and walks were tested, discarded and experimented anew. Vocal qualities, accents, lisps, stutters were lined up and tried out one by one. And of course, even the costume had to convey exactly what he wanted the character to express. A particular prop, such as a cigarette or monocle, might provide a starting point to a whole pattern of gestures. When all of these externals were assembled, the character would just seem to click into place, then the inner feelings would flow naturally. The hunchback, limping gait, facial sneer and simpering lilt that Olivier created for Richard III have become so identified with the part it is difficult to imagine it any other way.

FOOLING YOUR BRAIN

Neurophysiological data support the idea that body states can cause feelings. In studies by Paul Eckman, subjects were instructed to move their facial muscles in a specific way to compose an unstated emotional expression, the result being that they experienced a feeling appropriate to the expression.

For instance, a happy facial expression, though rough and incomplete, led to the subjects experiencing happiness, or anger, or surprise, or whatever.[4]

In the late 19th century, Carl Lange proposed a theory that stated that emotions are triggered by their physiological responses. One doesn't run because one is afraid, but one is afraid because one is running away from whatever the threatening event or object happens to be. Although this theory was since largely discredited, the discovery of neuro active chemicals puts it into a new light.[5]

Neurologist Dr. Oliver Sacks[6] found that by electrically stimulating a group of muscles, he could produce a feeling associated with the movement – for example, when twitching the shoulder into movement, he felt he was doing a Gallic shrug, complete with all the mental and feeling accompaniment of a French man making the gesture.

The tail wags the dog syndrome is described in a fascinating letter to the *Newsletter of the Schizophrenia Association of Great Britain (No. 30, Summer, 2000)*. The writer first takes the example of her own pet collie.

"I think the initial trigger (of the emotion) is a body sensation or reflex, which the brain receives and then interprets... With dogs you can literally see this happen – if you lift and wag a dog's tail for it, the front of the dog perks up and looks happy; if you tuck the tail down between the legs, the ears drop, etc., to match what it thinks it's feeling! It works on humans, too – this is how the Alexander Technique cures depression: train the body out of the depressive slump into a posture of happy, confident alertness, and this feeds back into the brain, and the biochemistry changes."

She then goes on to describe how a biochemical imbalance in her own body (which turned out to be an allergy to wheat) caused her to feel, just at the onset of a migraine, what she could only describe as a feeling of terror and a desire to flee from something hostile and evil. Although she understood intellectually that this was a brain phenomenon and that there was nothing to flee, her brain needed to make sense of her feelings and behaviour. It consequently searched for, and found, external things to be afraid of, and the woman became increasingly phobic, until diagnosed with severe agoraphobia and panic attacks. After 17 years of suffering, she tried cutting out wheat, and was instantly free of her attacks! Her description of the sense-seeking, confabulating brain makes it very clear how just throwing back your shoulders and puffing out your chest can fool the brain into inventing a reason – "Aha! That must be because she is feeling full of confidence." And bingo! You're confident!

The famous mirroring technique espoused by NLP is meant to build rapport with the client by subtly imitating his body posture and rhythms so that he unconsciously senses that you are like him, and so must be OK!

Antony Robbins will sometimes get volunteers in his class to experience this slightly differently. He will ask a first volunteer to sit in front of the class and to concentrate on an event that summons up strong emotions for him. The class then tries to guess the emotions, with limited success. Then a second volunteer comes up and mirrors his body position, his breathing, his facial expression – everything! Very rapidly he finds that, by adopting the same physical aspects he actually starts to feel the same feelings. He then describes out loud what he is feeling. I have tried this in a couple of my own classes and the accuracy is uncanny! Feeling elements that are completely overlooked or wrongly guessed when just observed are picked up and reproduced almost exactly through physical body position.

DECEPTION?

The big stumbling block in using this technique, deliberately adopting a stance or performing a gesture to produce a particular psychological effect, is the sense of fakery. We are so convinced that our gestures, to be genuine, must come from the heart, that to reverse the process seems to be dishonest or cheating. We need to understand that this reaction is an automatic defence mechanism. A very primitive part of our brain (sometimes called reptilian) reacts immediately to the unknown or unfamiliar as if it represents danger. It prefers routine and sameness, and is set up to preserve, as much as possible, the status quo. Consequently, any attempt at new behaviour which takes it out of the comfort zone will set up the alarm bells. You will find yourself saying, "This doesn't feel right!" And you will attribute this malaise to your higher, evolved spiritual nature, and a desire to aspire to truth – when, in fact, your primitive brain is prompting you! Have I convinced you?

If you find this shocking, good! I am doing my best to persuade you that your hesitations are based not so much on moral rectitude or the desire for authenticity, but on self-protection!

Fortunately, new behaviour and attitudes can be practised until they become familiar enough to feel right. Even happiness can be practised until it becomes a habit. As Maxwell Maltz says, "Happiness is a mental habit, a mental attitude, and if it is not learned and practised in the present it is never experienced."[7]

Even feelings of love, which we consider almost sacred as to their reality, can be stimulated and practised by initiating the necessary actions.

Some marriage guidance counsellors, when dealing with partners who no longer feel in love with their spouse, recommend this very procedure. They know that if the couple waits until their feelings come *before* they act, there is little hope for their relationship. "But, to act without the corresponding feelings seems dishonest, and they may be tired of pretending in the relationship. They want to be true to themselves. A very different approach is to act first and hope the feelings come later. This does not seem logical, but it works. You act *as if* you love the other person. You act *as if* you are in love with words and actions of affection. A very high percentage of people find, after days or weeks, they no longer have to act. Those feelings are true and sincere. The relationship is renewed."[8]

If you hesitate about pretending positive feelings of love and happiness, consider what happens when people pretend negative emotions like hatred and fear.

In an oft-quoted experiment carried out by Philip Zimbardo at Stanford University[9] students were asked to act out the roles of prison guards and prisoners. What started out as a sort of game, going through the motions, became so serious and intense that the experiment had to be called off. The guards were becoming genuinely brutal and vicious and the prisoners were slipping into frighteningly real depression and helplessness.

If tyrants and victims can be produced so rapidly in an experiment, when participants knew they were pretending, how much more is our society doing the same thing? How much of our personalities have been created because we have been, unaware, playing out roles forced upon us? And how much better, surely, to choose our own role?

The best way to be a new person is to start doing new things. At first, of course, any new actions will seem artificial, simply because you are not used to them. It is critical that you do not give up at this point, just because it doesn't feel right. You will need to make a conscious effort to keep up the role. If you persist, you will find that the new behaviour seems more and more natural, more and more *you*. With enough rehearsal, the subconscious identifies with the new role. Eventually the old *you* you have left behind may come to seem the artificial one.

DO IT!

So, decide who you want to be, how you want to be it, and then – *just do it*! Remember Miss Beckwith's advice at the beginning of this book. Start performing the actions. You will feel so much more in control of your life if you are an actor rather than a reactor. By reacting to circumstances, you remain a victim in life. Don't allow external events to dictate to you – "Be angry!" "Get upset!" "Be happy!" "Be sad!" You are not a robot following orders. You are a human being. Use your own free will. Choose to act.

Exercises

Exercise: BE AN IMPRESSIONIST – AND IMPRESS YOURSELF

Create a character you would like to play in a very specific situation – going to a meeting, an interview, a party or a date. Work on it as if you are an actor preparing a role. It can be completely invented, based on observation of another person, or a mixture of the two. Rehearse in front of a mirror. Try out different walks, gestures and facial expressions. Experiment with different vocal qualities and rhythms. Exaggerate, play around, have fun, until you have settled on a set of physical attributes. Go through your paces as this character in three or four different situations.

How would this character make an entrance?
How would he/she sit down in a chair? An armchair?
How would he/she use cutlery? Eat toast? Drink coffee?
How would he/she laugh? Tell jokes? Sneeze? Yawn?

Practise the mannerisms at home first, then in public when you are not with anyone – on a bus, walking in a park, attending a film or show alone.

Use the impressionists' technique of finding two or three tricks of physical position or movement that seem to switch on the character for you. Then, when you are ready for the actual situation, you just need to use these two or three triggers and the whole feeling you want to create will start flowing. Once connected, you can concentrate on the job at hand. You will already be in character and will not have to continue concentrating on how you are achieving it.

Exercise: LIFT UP YOUR BODY – AND YOUR SPIRITS!

1. To be happy

When you need to buck up your spirits, put a big smile on your face and open up your eyes wide. Stretch your neck up from your shoulders so your head feels buoyant. Instead of walking, skip. It's impossible to feel grumpy and skip at the same time. Hum to yourself a happy little song. Tap your feet. If possible, sing out loud, with gusto, something you associate with happiness, like "The Sunny Side of the Street". (Many of the Golden Oldies were written during the Great Depression for this exact purpose!)

2. To be energetic and enthusiastic

Stand up straight, with your spine and head in a vertical line. Fling your arms outward and back again to your chest as you take in big gulps of air. Run on the spot, lifting your knees high in the air. Say out loud, "Wow! Fantastic! Great!" Sound as if you mean it.

3. To be confident

Take a tip from professional dancers, who always give out an air of confidence and self-esteem. Stand tall, walk tall, with your spine stretched and your head held high. If you place your head slightly back with your chin tucked a little inwards rather than protruding forward, the cranium will be better balanced on the atlas bone, the first of the cervical vertebrae. You may feel as if you are looking down your nose. Stay with it, and not only will you feel more confident within yourself, but you will come across better to others.

After an acting class in Australia, where we studied how head position indicated high or low status, one of my girlfriends decided to try out acting high status in the front bar of the local pub. She was amazed to find that, whereas she was usually ignored and felt nonexistent, this time she was treated with respect, people paid attention to her, listened avidly to what she had to say and even insisted on buying her drinks!

"All I did," she said, bewildered by her newfound social success, "was to hold my head up and keep it still!" She had found her physical switch, or trigger, to turn on self-confidence.

Conclusion

CHAPTER 13

Curtain Up!

So here we are already – the end of the book! What happens now? Do you put the book back on the shelf, saying, "That was really interesting," and do nothing about it? Do you lend it to a friend, saying, "You'll love this!" – and still do nothing about it? Or do you decide, now, to put it into action? If you have been practising some of the exercises at the end of each chapter, then you are already well on the way.

If not, now is the moment to start. Don't shut the pages of this book until you have made the commitment to experiment with one of the exercises, or invent your own, to practise being who you want to be.

Here is a reminder of what you can do....

Chapter 2

FINDING YOUR VOICE
Pretend to be your favourite singer(s) and discover your vocal possibilities.

PLAY A NEW ROLE
When nobody knows you, escape from preconceived ideas and be someone else.

Chapter 3

WAKE UP WITH ANTICIPATION
A morning energiser: Be a child again and decide what game you will play today.

YOU'RE A STAR!
Imagine yourself as the star of the film, dealing with situations in your life.

Chapter 4

JOIN UP A GROUP
Take part in a play and develop your acting skills.

REINVENT YOURSELF
Do something different that is not normally *you.*

MENTAL REHEARSAL No.1
Prepare for an event with a mental run-through. Imagine you are someone else who has the quality you need.

Chapter 5

BE YOUR OWN HERO
Play a different hero everyday. Practise their heroic qualities.

PRETEND YOU CAN'T OPEN YOUR EYES
Use self-hypnosis for positive suggestions.
Hypnotise yourself to stay as you want to be, as long as you are pretending.

Chapter 6

MULTIPLE YOUS
Look back over your life to find the patterns and re-connect with the aspects of your personality that would help you now.

Chapter 7

TOTEM ANIMALS
Allow an archetypal animal to emerge from each body chakra. Call them to a powwow.

MEET YOURSELVES
Ask the conflicting parts of you to express themselves. Negotiate a solution.

Chapter 8

PAST LIFE TALENT
Daydream being in a past life to connect with a creative gift that you want to develop.

YOUR SOUL'S DESIRE
Take a trip back in time to before you were born to re-discover why you chose to come – your mission in life.

Chapter 9

AWARENESS
Watch yourself, as an outside observer, and catch yourself playing roles from habit.

WHICH HAT?
Switch thinking styles from one extreme to another to stimulate creativity.

INFINITE DIMENSIONS
Visit yourself in another dimension, where you are the expert who can help and advise you.

Chapter 10

MENTAL REHEARSAL, No.2
Create a new self-image and practise it mentally over and over, living all the details in advance.

ON STAGE!
In three scenes, understudy a role model, watch yourself try out the part, and then make it your own.

Chapter 11

START SMALL
Just for one day, ask yourself, "What if...?" and try it.

IF I WERE ALREADY...
Project yourself into the future goal already achieved. Look back from this standpoint in time.

Chapter 12

IMPRESS YOURSELF
Create a whole new character and learn how to switch it on with a single gesture.

LIFT UP YOUR BODY – AND YOUR SPIRITS!
Put your body in the physical position it would have if experiencing the desired emotions.

Most important to remember is that you don't *have* to believe something is true for it to come true. So many thousands have denied themselves a happier, more fulfilled existence because they have been hung up on the idea that to be a genuine person they must cultivate a genuine belief. But affirmations repeated dozens of times a day will not necessarily create a genuine belief. They may even compound the problem!

Telling yourself, "I AM sick, BUT I believe I will get well," may actually exacerbate the conflict between current reality and the desired belief, and create even bigger barriers. On the contrary, acting AS IF you are already cured makes barriers vanish away. [1]

YOUR REAL POTENTIAL

There is a clever ad for a beer that "reaches parts the others don't reach". Well, *pretending* can reach parts of you, deep down, that other belief systems and affirmations can't reach. When you make believe, you release parts that are *already* there in you, as undeveloped potential. And you have the potential to be *all things*. As a human being, you are potentially everything that any human can do, be or act.

So, next time you find yourself reiterating a positive statement that you don't quite believe, can you just *pretend* it's true? That way, you can be your best potential every day, not just when you feel equal to it.

At first, it may seem like you're not being authentic. It's just because it's new and different. All of us prefer something that is routine and comfortable, even if it is damaging us in the long run. You can help the unknown become more familiar, and thus more accessible, through the magic of make believe.

And finally, to quote Robert Dilts, "What's the difference between pretending and really changing? If you pretend long enough, it will seem as real as anything else." [2]

I was discussing with Lila, my collaborator for the French version of this book, why pretending has such a bad reputation. We talked about how many people invented artificial roles because they lacked a sense of identity and were desperately searching for one outside of themselves. The sense of *not me* is particularly bewildering when there is no *me* to balance it.

This technique of Make Believe is not meant to fill in an empty hole with an unsubstantial fantasy. On the contrary, its value lies in allowing the true self to evolve beyond the artificial barriers imposed by external limits.

We found that the two of us, Lila and myself, shared a common factor in our own role playing. No matter how many different costumes we wore, we never lost our central sense of identity, the knowledge of our Inner Being that never changes.

This led me to chunk up a few levels, musing about how that Inner Being within us all could be likened to God, who was Himself [3] playing different roles. Although manifest in all things, He never loses his sense of identity.

"I like that, said Lila. "Put that in you your last chapter."

So, here it is.

If the Universe is the Creation of God,
then it is the Expression of God.

The Magic of Make Believe

I like to imagine God AS IF he is the Master Actor of the Universe. Having written the script, (as Master Playwright of the Universe) he is now playing the whole of Creation – an infinite variety of different roles – acting out a forest, a tree, a leaf, an ocean, a river, a bubble, a water drop – the whole vast expanse of Nature. In this make believe scenario, God would be bored just Being for eternity, so he plays, endlessly inventing new games and new roles for his own delight.

And perhaps His greatest delight is playing human beings, when he pretends to forget Himself, just temporarily, by becoming so involved in his role, playing each single human being as a totally unique and individual expression of Himself – with the addition of self-consciousness, so that He can also be his own audience at the same time that He is performing!

It was Shakespeare who created the original concept of Hamlet, but hundreds of different actors have incarnated the role, each in their own particular, personal style, from the melancholy intellectual of Laurence Olivier to the frustrated man-of-action of Mel Gibson (Mad Max!)

Just so, on a cosmic level, God created the concept of Humanity in His own image, then proceeded, as Casting Agent of the Universe, to hand out the role to billions of different versions of Himself; for his own infinite satisfaction and pleasure in the discovery of Himself.

Of course, I couldn't possibly know about any of this, but I can make believe! What fun if you were God, pretending to be You!

So, whatever your personal beliefs about the Life Force, and your unique expression of it, be aware that the Stage Manager is calling for "Beginners on stage, please." Check your costume and makeup. The show is about to begin. Now playing is the Game of Life, and you are starring in the lead role of ... (your name here, in lights!)

Enjoy yourself! Be brilliant!
Curtain up!

Appendices

ENDNOTES

Chapter 2: Acting My Life

1. The huge popularity of the Harry Potter books is partly due to the fact that so many children can identify with him, a typical schoolchild coping with everyday growing problems, who at the same time is discovering his magical powers.
2. "Persona" is the Latin word for mask.
3. From a conversation with Dale B. Taylor, director of music therapy studies, University of Wisconsin.

Chapter 3: Childhood

1. Jean Piaget, *The Psychology of the Child* Basic Books, 1969, 2000.
2. Carla Hannaford, *Smart Moves: Why Learning is not All in Your Head,* Great Ocean Publishers (Paperback)
3. *New Scientist*, 27th January 2001, No. 2275.
4. *Les Vilains Petits Canards*, 2002, *Le Murmure des Fantômes*, 2003, Odile Jacob. *The Whispering of Ghosts*, 2004.
5. Interview in *Psychologies* magazine, September 2002 (my translation).
6. Bruno Bettelheim, *The Uses of Enchantment: The Meaning and Importance of Fairy Tales*, Vintage Books, 1989.

Chapter 4: Theatre

1. Jacques Falguières, "Le Théâtre retrouve sa Voix," *Paris-Normandie,* 2001.
2. We will see later how theatre can be used as a therapy, an aid to personal development and a means of spiritual enlightenment.
3. Mihalyi Csikszentmihalyi, *Flow: The Psychology of Optimal Experience.* New York, Harper & Row.
4. *ADVANCES: The Journal of Mind-Body Health*, vol.10, No.4, Fall 1994.
5. This will be explained in Chapter 6, part IIIA.
6. It appears Hillary Clinton herself used Eleanor Roosevelt as a role-model. When in doubt, she would ask herself, "What would Eleanor do in this situation?"
7. Mental rehearsal with a role model is one of the secrets of top sportsmen.

Endnotes

For a more fully developed form of this technique, see the exercise ON STAGE, chapter 10, ROLE PLAYING.

Chapter 5: Hypnosis

1. Dave Elman, p.26, *Hypnotherapy*, 1964, Westwood Publishing Co.
2. p. 306, *Ibid*.
3. pp.11-14, *Mind Matters*, Michael S. Gazzaniga, 1988.
4. p.55, "Basic Hypnotherapy", student manual, National Guild of Hypnotists.
5. Ormond McGill passed away in October 2005. I had the honour of being a participant in his last stage show.
6. p.27, Dave Elman.
7. p.34, Ibid.
8. Developed by Charles Tebbetts and Roy Hunter.

Chapter 6: Multiple Personality Syndrome

1. *Diagnostic and Statistical Manual of Mental Disorders, IV*.
2. Joan A. Turkus, MD, www.dissociation.co.uk
3. This is NOT schizophrenia, which is often mislabeled "split personality".
4. *The Three Faces of Eve*, Corgett Thigpenn, 1957. *A Mind of My Own*, Christine Costner Sizemore, 1989, autobiography of the original patient known as "Eve".
5. *Sybil*, Flora Rheta Schreiber, 1974, 1989, Mass Market Paperback.
6. *When Rabbit Howls*, Truddi Chase, 1987.
7. "Transformation of the Personality and the Immune System," Nicholas R.S. Hall, Maureen O'Grady and Denis Calandra (*The Journal of Mind-Body Health*, volume 10, no.4, Fall 1994.)
8. *The Holographic Universe*, Michael Talbot, 1991, Perrenial.
9. P.5, *Imagery for Getting Well*, Deidre Davis Brigham, 1994, W.W.Nortin & Company.
10. Talbot, p. 100.

Chapter 7: Discovering Your Parts

1. *Psycho-Drama*, vols. 1-3, J.L. Moreno, MD (1889 -1974), Beacon Press 1972.
2. Robert Brodie, ANZ Psychodrama Association, www.users.on.net

3. Quoted on www.zambula.demon.co.uk/schools/sociodrama
4. *Embracing Our Selves,* Hal Stone and Sidra Winkelman, 1985, De Vorss.
5. *Miracles on Demand*, Charles Tebbetts, (out of print).
6. www.royhunter.com
7. Workshop Notes, © 2002, C. Roy Hunter, NGH Summer Institute, 2003.
8. Article reprinted in Workshop Notes, *Ibid.*
9. This connection with Higher Wisdom seems to be part of a growing trend in Hypnotherapy moving away from the classic power position of the hypnotist.
10. Jerry Seavey, www.mindbridge.cc

Chapter 8: Past Lives

1. Film actress known for her New Age views on past lives, spirit channelling, etc., especially in her book, *Dancing in the Light,* 1986, Bantam Books.
2. *Many Lives, Many Masters,* Brian Weiss, MD, 1988, Simon and Schuster.
3. *Past Lives, Future Lives*, Dr. Bruce Goldberg, 1988, Ballantyne Books.

Chapter 9: Infinite Variety

1. *Frogs into Princes*, p.160, Richard Bandler and John Grinder, Real People Press, 1979.
2. *Six Thinking Hats*, p. 29, Edward de Bono, 1986, Viking.
3. "The Doubling Theory," J.P. Garnier-Malet, *International Journal of Computing Anticipatory Systems*, Belgium, 1998: vol.2, 1999: vol. 3, 5 & 10. www.garnier-malet.com.
4. From SuperMind and Parallel Dimension Quest. www.burtgoldman.com

Chapter 10: Role Play

1. I have a great respect for synchronicity, so I would like to report that, while I am typing these words, I am listening to a song I've never heard before: *"You're always waiting for somebody, and you don't like yourself. They made you change the you, you remember when you were someone else.*
2. *Six Thinking Hats,* page 20, Edward de Bono, Viking, 1985, 1986.
3. *Journal of Personality and Social Psychology,* November 2003.
4. *The Luck Factor*, Dr. Richard Wiseman, 2003, London, Century.

Endnotes

Chapter 11: The Magic Word "If"

1. *The Structure of Magic, A Book about Language and Therapy,* Richard Bandler and John Grinder, 1975, Science and Behaviour Books.
2. *I Could Do Anything, If I Only Knew What It Was,* Barbara Sher with Barbara Smith, pages 21, 22. 1994, Dell Publishing.
3. *Essentials of Hypnosis,* Michael D. Yapko, PhD. p. 97, 1995, Brunner/Mazel.
4. *Frogs into Princes, Neuro Linguistic Programming,* Richard Bandler and John Grinder, p. 168. 1979, Real People Press.
5. *Essentials of Hypnosis,* p.60, *Ibid.*
6. *Influencing with Integrity,* Genie Z. Laborde, p.147-8, 1984, Syntony Publishing.
7. p.148-9, *Ibid.*
8. *Psycho-Cybernetics,* Maxwell Maltz, 1960. Prentice-Hall.

Chapter 12: Action!

1. *Six Thinking Hats,* Edward de Bono, p.6,18, 1985, Viking.
2. *Psycho-Cybernetics,* Maxwell Maltz, 1960, Prentice-Hall.
3. "Notes on How an Actor Prepares," *NEA Higher Education: Advocate* online – www.nea.org/he
4. "Facial Expressions of Emotion: New Findings, New Questions,*" Psychological Science,* Paul Ekman, 1992, 4:342-45.
5. *ADVANCES: The Journal of Mind-Body Health,* vol.10. no.4, Fall 1994.
6. Known especially for his most famous book, *The Man who Mistook his Wife for a Hat, and Other Clinical Tales,* Oliver Sacks, 1998, Touchstone Books.
7. Psycho-Cybernetics, p. 98, *Ibid.*
8. www.ourtimehas.com/marriage
9. *The Stanford Prison Experiment,* Philip Zimbardo, 1971, Stanford University, www.prisonexp.org

Chapter 13: Curtain Up!

1. This does *not* mean, of course, interrupting medical treatment!
2. *Beliefs, Pathways to Health and Well-being,* Robert Dilts, Tim Hallborn and Suzi Smith, p.43, 1990, Metamorphous Press.
3. He could equally be She, or He/She. I just don't conceive of God as "It".

BIBLIOGRAPHY

ADVANCES: The Journal of Mind-Body Health, vol.10, No.4, Fall 1994.

Bandler, Richard, and Grinder, John, *Frogs into Princes, Neuro Linguistic Programming,* Real People Press, 1979.

Bandler, Richard, and Grinder, John, *The Structure of Magic, A Book about Language and Therapy,* Science and Behaviour Books, 1975.

Berne, Eric, *Games People Play: The Psychology of Human Relationships,* 1964, Ballantyne Books, 1996.

Bettelheim, Bruno, *The Uses of Enchantment: The Meaning and Importance of Fairy Tales,* Vintage Books, 1989.

Brigham, Deidre Davis, *Imagery for Getting Well,* W.W.Nortin & Company, 1994.

Chase, Truddi, *When Rabbit Howls,* E P Dutton, 1987.

Csikszentmihalyi, Mihalyi, *Flow: The Psychology of Optimal Experience,* New York, Harper & Row, 1990.

Cyrulnik, Boris, *The Whispering of Ghosts,* Other Press, 2004.

De Bono, Edward, *Six Thinking Hats,* Viking, 1986.

De Ropp, Robert S. *The Master Game, Pathways to Higher Consciousness,* Consciousness Classics, 1968.

Diagnostic and Statistical Manual of Mental Disorders, Fourth Edition, DSM-IV, American Psychiatric Association, 1994.

Dilts, Robert; Hallborn, Tim; and Smith, Suzi, *Beliefs, Pathways to Health and Well-being,* Metamorphous Press, 1990.

Elman, Dave, *Hypnotherapy,* Westwood Publishing Co., 1964.

Gazzaniga, Michael S. *Mind Matters,* Houghton Mifflin, 1988.

Goldberg, Dr. Bruce, *Past Lives, Future Lives,* Ballantyne Books, 1988.

Hall, Nicholas R.S., O'Grady, Maureen and Calandra, Denis, *Transformation of the Personality and the Immune System,* (ADVANCES: The Journal of Mind-Body Health, volume 10, no.4, Fall 1994.).

Hannaford, Dr. Carla, *Smart Moves:* Why Learning is not All in Your Head, Great Ocean Publishers, Paperback, 1995.

Laborde, Genie Z., *Influencing with Integrity,* Syntony Publishing, 1984.

Maclaine, Shirley, *Dancing in the Light,* Bantam Books, 1986.

Maltz, Maxwell, *Psycho-Cybernetics,* Prentice-Hall, 1960.

Moreno, J.L., MD, *Psycho-Drama,* vols. 1-3, Beacon Press, 1972.

Piaget, Jean, *The Psychology of the Child,* Basic Books, 1969, 2000.

Bibliography

The Schizophrenia Association of Great Britain, Newsletter
(No. 30, Summer, 2000).

Schreiber, Flora Rheta, *Sybil,* Mass Market Paperback, 1974, 1989.

Sacks, Oliver, *The Man who mistook his Wife for a Hat, and other Clinical Tales,* Touchstone Books, 1998.

Sher, Barbara, with Smith, Barbara, *I could do Anything, if I only knew what it was,* Dell Publishing, 1994.

Sizemore, Christine Costner, *A Mind of my Own,* William Morrow & Co., 1989.

Stanislavsky, Constantin, *An Actor Prepares,* Theatre Arts, 1936, Routledge, 1989.

Stone, Hal, and Winkelman, *Sidra, Embracing Our Selves,* De Vorss, 1985.

Talbot, Michael, *The Holographic Universe,* Perrenial, 1991.

Thigpenn, Corgett, *The Three Faces of Eve,* 1957.

Tebbetts , Charles, *Miracles on Demand,* (out of print).

Weiss, Brian, MD, *Many Lives, Many Masters,* Simon and Schuster, 1988.

Wiseman, Dr. Richard, *The Luck Factor,* London, Century, 2003.

Yapko, Michael D., PhD., *Essentials of Hypnosis,* Brunner/Mazel, 1995.

Zimbardo, Philip, *The Stanford Prison Experiment,* www.prisonexp.org, Stanford University , 1971.

ACKNOWLEDGEMENTS

To all my "teachers" – (Burt Goldman, Jerry and Marilou Seavey, José Silva and his family, Richard Harte, Gerald Kein, Don Mottin, and many others)

To all my colleagues in the National Guild of Hypnotists (USA), Silva International (USA) and Professional Speakers Association (UK)

To everybody mentioned in this book, for their words and their inspiration

To all my students, who continue to teach me beyond what I have learned from my teachers

To my original French editors, Catherine Maillard et Claudia Trédaniel

To Lila Veronese, my collaborator for the French language version

To both my families: Mum, Anne and Fern in Australia: Ena and Peg in England.

To Michael, my husband, for his unique and unquestioning support.

Thankyou, everybody!

For further information, and to contact Lee Pascoe:

Central web-site: www.leepascoe.com
E-mail: lee.pascoe@lamethodesilva.com,
or lee@hypnovision.net
Telephone (France) 33 2 32 34 45 42

FINDHORN Press

Books, Card Sets,
CDs & DVDs
that inspire and uplift

For a complete catalogue,
please contact:

Findhorn Press Ltd
305a The Park, Findhorn
Forres IV36 3TE
Scotland, UK

Telephone
+44-(0)1309-690582
Fax
+44(0)1309-690036
eMail
info@findhornpress.com

or consult our catalogue online
(with secure order facility) on

www.findhornpress.com